The Visual Dictionary of Typography

academia

An AVA Book

Published by AVA Publishing SA
Rue des Fontenailles 16
Case Postale
1000 Lausanne 6
Switzerland
Tel: +41 786 005 109
Email: enquiries@avabooks.com

Distributed by Thames & Hudson (ex-North America)
181a High Holborn
London WC1V 7QX
United Kingdom
Tel: +44 20 7845 5000
Fax: +44 20 7845 5055
Email: sales@thameshudson.co.uk
www.thamesandhudson.com

Distributed in the USA & Canada by:
Ingram Publisher Services Inc.
1 Ingram Blvd.
La Vergne TN 37086
USA
Tel: +1 866 400 5351
Fax: +1 800 838 1149
Email: customer.service@ingrampublisherservices.com

English Language Support Office
AVA Publishing (UK) Ltd.
Tel: +44 1903 204 455
Email: enquiries@avabooks.com

ISBN 978-2-940411-18-4

10 9 8 7 6 5 4 3 2 1

Design by Gavin Ambrose
www.gavinambrose.co.uk

Production by AVA Book Production Pte. Ltd., Singapore
Tel: +65 6334 8173
Fax: +65 6259 9830
Email: production@avabooks.com.sg

Gavin Ambrose & Paul Harris

The Visual Dictionary of Typography

academia

This book is an easy-to-use reference to the key terms used in typography. Each entry comprises a brief textual definition along with an illustration or visual example of the point under discussion. Supplementary contextual information is also provided.

Key areas addressed in this book are those terms commonly used in reference to the study of typography.

Entries are presented in alphabetical order to provide an easy reference system.

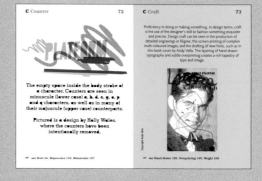

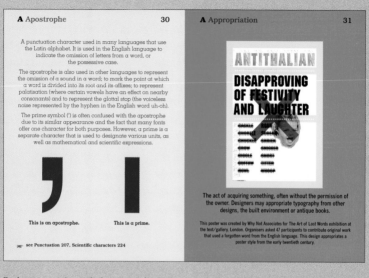

A Apostrophe 30

A punctuation character used in many languages that use the Latin alphabet. It is used in the English language to indicate the omission of letters from a word, or the possessive case.

The apostrophe is also used in other languages to represent the omission of a sound in a word; to mark the point at which a word is divided into its root and its affixes; to represent palatisation (where certain vowels have an effect on nearby consonants) and to represent the glottal stop (the voiceless noise represented by the hyphen in the English word uh-oh).

The prime symbol (') is often confused with the apostrophe due to its similar appearance and the fact that many fonts offer one character for both purposes. However, a prime is a separate character that is used to designate various units, as well as mathematical and scientific expressions.

This is an apostrophe.   This is a prime.

☞ see Punctuation 207, Scientific characters 224

A Appropriation 31

The act of acquiring something, often without the permission of the owner. Designers may appropriate typography from other designs, the built environment or antique books.

This poster was created by Why Not Associates for The Art of Lost Words exhibition at the text/gallery, London. Organisers asked 47 participants to contribute original work that used a forgotten word from the English language. This design appropriates a poster style from the early twentieth century.

Each page contains a single entry and, where appropriate, a printer's hand symbol ☞ provides page references to other related and relevant entries.

276

**1st Century BC
Etruscan**
The development of the carved letterform begins with the Etruscan, and later Roman carvers working in marble. This period saw the development of stroke variation and changes in the vertical weight and proportion of characters.

**150 BC
Paper**
Paper was invented in China in 150 BC and is considered one of the Four Great Inventions of Ancient China, along with the compass, gunpowder and printing. Paper was a cheap alternative to silk and allowed for the production of printed items. Consequently, it also meant that China could export more silk (as it wasn't being used for a writing surface) and this lead to increased wealth and prosperity. Around this time, early paper mills were formed in China and Japan, and the use of paper spread around the world (although it didn't reach Europe for nearly 900 years).

**1150–1500
Black letter**
Black letter is a form of script in common usage throughout Europe (though most notably in Germany where it was in use for over 500 years). Also called Textura, relating to the woven appearance it made on a page, Black letter has several variants. Rotunda is a more open character variety common in Southern Europe. Bastarde, a mix of Black letter and Rotunda was common in England, France and parts of Northern Europe. Although we now perceive it as hard to read, it was in its day considered perfectly legible.

277

**1170–c.1250
Fibonacci numbers**
The Fibonacci number sequence is named after Leonardo of Pisa, who was also known as Fibonacci. His number series is constructed with each number being the sum of the previous two. The sequence can be used to create a sense of harmony and proportion to a design. The sequence, starting at 0 is as follows:

0, 1, 1, 2, 3, 5, 8 13, 21, 34, 55, 89, 144...

These numbers might be used when designing grids, or when selecting appropriate proportional relationships between type sizes, for example.

**c.1398–1468
Johannes Gutenberg**
A printer who is credited with developing the first printing press and movable type. Although it is known that other nations and printers had done similar exercises, it was his persistence that led to the widespread use of printing in this way. His system used a 'casting' of individual letterforms that could be reused. He also created an ink with sufficient 'tack' to stick effectively to these metal forms.

**1436
Movable type**
A system of printing that used individually, when formed characters to create lines, paragraphs, and pages of text. The characters could be set, used, dismantled and reused, leading to a cost-effective way of printing en masse. This form of printing was extensively used well into the twentieth century. Many printing terms in use today are a reference to this technology. For example leading, a term used today to describe the space between lines of type, which, in movable type, was formed of thin slithers of metal.

A timeline helps to provide historical context for selected key moments in the development and evolution of typography.

Introduction

Welcome to *The Visual Dictionary of Typography*,
a book that provides textual definitions and visual
explanations for common terms found in typography
and related disciplines.

This book aims to provide a clear understanding of the
many terms used within typography and graphic design.
As you might expect, visual explanations and
examples from key graphic design studios are given,
from the traditional and the classic to the contemporary
and experimental.

Left: This book cover was
created by Andy Vella and
features sans serif typography
to create a youthful visual
impression. The text is styled
to appear as though it has been
burnt into the wood, which adds
a rawness that is in keeping
with the subject matter. Image
copyright Andy Vella.

Opposite: This staff booklet,
by To The Point for Moneycorp,
demonstrates the clarity of a
simple, enforced hierarchy.
Hierarchy is discussed on
page 130.

"mighty oaks from little acorns grow"

WHAT DOES IT MEAN FOR YOU?

With a fantastic, brand refresh and exciting new corporate direction, TTT Moneycorp is in a great place to build...

Outstanding career op...

A **rock solid** co...

A **fun** —

A NEW BEGINNING

It has been almost 30 years since the first TTT branch opened for business on Oxford Street. As Geoffrey Chaucer wrote in the 1370's, "mighty oaks from little acorns grow" and such has been the case for TTT Moneycorp, with the business experiencing of all amazing growth thanks to the hard work and dedication of all who work here.

My warmest thanks to each and every one of you!

Bassam

Bassam Shlewet, Chairman

A BRAND FOR THE FUTURE

As much as we'd love to implement the new this business immediate... the sheer size... this impossible. Therefore the new bra... over the coming months. You will be... progress by email and the ini...

But as of today, please answer ...

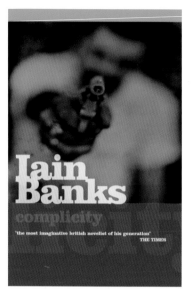

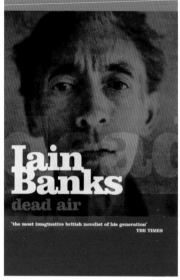

Above:
These book covers created
by Andy Vella feature
negative leading and slab
serifs to produce a solid-
looking block of type.
Leading is discussed on
page 149. Image copyright
Andy Vella.

Left:
This brochure created
by Unthink features a
headline with negative
leading overprinting a
dramatic image. Headlines
are discussed on page
178, and overprinting
on page 190.

Right:
This CD artwork was
created by Frost Design
for Sheesham and Lotus.
It features a tapestry
of letterpress typography
sizes and typefaces to
represent the oldtime,
ragtime and folk music
the record contains.
Letterpress is discussed
on page 153.

Typography communicates through a range of visual
devices, from words constructed by a chain of letters to
messages formed by the visual appearance of letters on
a page.

A clear understanding of the key terms and concepts
used in typography will enable you to better articulate
and formalise ideas, and will ensure greater accuracy
in your communication of those ideas to others.

With the benefit of technological developments,
the field of typography is flourishing and represents a
powerful, vibrant and constantly evolving and expanding
applied visual form. It is a media with a long history
and noble heritage, but it is also a vital, dynamic and
contemporary means of expression, interpretation and
communication, which conveys ideas and messages
with compelling form in any media.

The following text provides thought-provoking, compact and basic definitions, and instructive insights into important fundamental principles, methods, materials, equipment, technical advances, techniques and movements in typography and art and design.

The book also includes a timeline charting the evolution of and developments in the field of typography and covers work by such notable figures as William Caxton, Johannes Gutenberg, Giambattista Bodoni and John Baskerville.

Left:
Texture can add to the visual impact of typography. Texture is discussed on page 250.

Opposite:
This experimental design by The Zek Crew features a re-invention of the serif, with dots used rather than glyphs. Serifs are discussed on page 226 and glyphs on page 117.

THE ZEK CREW

THE
ZEK
CREW

Contents

The Dictionary

Abbreviations are formed by omitting the end of a word or words. Contractions (formed by omitting the middle of a word or words) and acronyms (formed from the initial letters of words) are also forms of abbreviation.

Abbreviations present a typographical challenge in terms of achieving consistency, conveying the required, unequivocal meaning and producing a clean design. Rules regarding the use of upper-/lower-case letters and full points vary widely so in terms of typography, consistency and convenience are the most important factors. Variations in UK English include:

A.M. vs am (a contraction of antemeridian)
Prof. vs Prof (an abbreviation of Professor)

Acronyms never carry full points. For example:
NASA (National Aeronautics and Space Administration)

☞ see Acronyms 21, Minuscules 167

A CONCEPT OR IDEA THAT IS NOT ASSOCIATED WITH ANYTHING SPECIFIC. PEOPLE GIVE MEANING TO ABSTRACT DESIGNS BY COGNITIVELY APPLYING WHAT THEY HAVE LEARNED FROM THE IMPLIED AND LITERAL MEANINGS OF OTHER THINGS.

THIS DESIGN BY FUTRO FEATURES TYPOGRAPHY THAT HAS BEEN ABSTRACTED THROUGH THE USE OF FILLED COUNTERS, ZERO TRACKING AND LETTER SPACING. THIS ABSTRACTION MAKES THE WORDS MORE DIFFICULT TO READ, BUT CREATES A STRONG, ABSTRACT VISUAL STATEMENT.

☞ see Counter 72, Denotive and cognitive meaning 79

Various diacritical marks indicate how the sound of a letter is modified when pronounced. Accents are rarely used in English but are relatively common in other languages. Pictured below are the main accents used in European languages, together with their common names in English. They are available for lower case, upper case and small capitals. Standard fonts include some letters that have accents already positioned above them, but it may sometimes be necessary to construct these manually. To do this, position the accent (a glyph) after the letter and kern it back until it is correctly positioned.

é	É	Acute	č	Č	Háček
ő	Ő	Double acute	ā	Ā	Macron
è	È	Grave	ç	Ç	Cedilla
ê	Ê	Circumflex	ą	Ą	Ogonek
ë	Ë	Umlaut / diaeresis	å	Å	Ring
ă	Ă	Breve	ä	Ä	Umlaut
ñ	Ñ	Tilde	ȧ	Ȧ	Dot / Overdot

☞ see Glyphs 117, Kerning 143, Overdot 189, Small capitals 235

An abbreviation formed using the initial letters of a phrase or name. Acronyms are pronounced as words themselves. For example:

NASA, NATO, UEFA, Aga, Fiat, scuba, laser

Acronyms do not take full points and may be set in small capitals as shown below:

The U.S. government plans to send a manned spacecraft to the moon. The NASA is tasked with making this happen.

(1) Small caps generated by layout software – notice the lighter small capitals

The U.S. government plans to send a manned spacecraft to the moon. The NASA is tasked with making this happen.

(2) Specific small caps cut of the original font – notice the matched font weights

☞ see **Abbreviations** 18, **Small capitals** 235

The horizontal position of type within a text block.

Centred
Centred aligns each line horizontally in the centre to form a symmetrical shape on the page. Line beginnings and endings are ragged. Raggedness can be controlled to a certain extent by adjusting line endings.

Justified
Justified text sees each line extend from the left to right margin by varying the space between words and breaking them. This can allow the appearance of rivers of white space___and___plagues___of hyphenation to appear.

Range right
Flush right, ragged left alignment sees the text aligned to the right. This arrangement is less common as it is more difficult to read, but is sometimes used for picture captions and other accompanying texts as it is clearly distinct from body copy.

Range left
Flush left, ragged right alignment follows the principle of handwriting, with text tight and aligned to the left margin and ending ragged on the right.

F   o   r   c   e   d
Forced alignment is similar to justified but each line is forced to extend fully between the right and left margins, even short lines of text. Forced is rarely used but can sometimes be seen in newspaper copy.

☞ see Rivers 217, Text blocks 246

A set of letters, characters or symbols used to write or represent a language. Most alphabets represent consonant and vowel sounds. However, in some systems, symbols are used to represent whole words. Egyptian hieroglyphs are an example of these non-alphabetic representations. Most modern-day European alphabets are derived from the modern Latin alphabet (a descendant of the Phoenician alphabet). The modern Latin alphabet consists of 52 upper-case and lower-case letters, with ten numerals and a variety of other symbols. However, different languages use various combinations of these.

The Phoenician alphabet is derived from ancient Egyptian hieroglyphs and some of the symbols are shown here. Each letter's name begins with the letter itself, and in many cases, the symbols represent the objects they are named after.

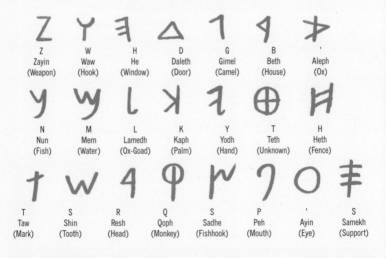

Z	W	H	D	G	B	'
Zayin	Waw	He	Daleth	Gimel	Beth	Aleph
(Weapon)	(Hook)	(Window)	(Door)	(Camel)	(House)	(Ox)

N	M	L	K	Y	T	H
Nun	Mem	Lamedh	Kaph	Yodh	Teth	Heth
(Fish)	(Water)	(Ox-Goad)	(Palm)	(Hand)	(Unknown)	(Fence)

T	S	R	Q	S	P	'	S
Taw	Shin	Resh	Qoph	Sadhe	Peh	Ayin	Samekh
(Mark)	(Tooth)	(Head)	(Monkey)	(Fishhook)	(Mouth)	(Eye)	(Support)

☞ see Arabic 32

Lack of clarity or definition. Ambiguity exists where it is unclear how to interpret or identify different letters in a text block.

Put simply, some fonts are easier to read than others. But equally you can argue that readability is related to context. The font below, for example, would be hard to read set as small body copy, but would be perfectly legible in a heading or fairground signage.

It is worth considering the priorities of a piece of typography. Whether it needs to be engaging, or readable, or distinct, will inform the typographical outcome.

☞ see Font/Typeface 106, Legibility 151, Readability 210

A ligature of the letters of the Latin word *et*, which
means 'and'.

The earliest usage of the ampersand symbol dates back
to the first century AD and it is now found in many
languages that use the Latin alphabet. The provenance
of the ampersand can be clearly seen in some typefaces
where the E and T can be distinguished.

The ampersand is presented in all manner of ways in
different typefaces, as the above examples show.

☞ see Punctuation 207

The different strokes that form typographical characters. Each letter can be thought of as a body comprised of various constituent parts, and the study and identification of these parts likened to anatomy.

Various non-alphabetic typographic characters.
Ancillary characters are used to communicate different
ideas or concepts and add further understanding to
text. Such characters include punctuation marks,
symbols, pictograms and modified letterforms.
Ancillary alphabetic characters can be classified into
the following general groups:

Single stroke symbols, punctuation and diacritical marks made
with a single mark or stroke:

o   ∧   –   .   [|

Double stroke symbols, punctuation and diacritical marks made
with two marks or strokes:

«   "   :   ;   +   =

Multiple stroke symbols, punctuation and mathematical characters:

...   %   ±   ÷   §

Pictograms symbols, punctuation and decorative elements:

‡   *

Modified letterforms ligatures, signs and other punctuation
with historical letterform origins:

§   &   £   Æ   Ø   Œ

A sequence of images that are displayed one after the other in quick succession to give the appearance of movement. Animation has become popular in graphic design due to an extension of the media that designers work with, and the innovations of web and digital communications. Working in the digital sphere and using programs such as Flash allows text and images to be animated. Animating text helps to draw user attention and can augment and reflect the personality of a brand in the way that it moves. Animation is also used to produce opening titles and idents in TV and film production.

The stills shown here are from an animation created by Social Design for Universal Music's Sam King. The animation features an 'o' in the form of an exploding CD.

see Moving image 172

ZOV
AR

The point formed at the top of a character such as 'A' where the left and right strokes meet. Some typefaces have exaggerated pointed apexes, while others are softer and rounded.

This logo was created by Faydherbe/de Vringer for ZOVAR (Zorgverzekeraars identificatie en authenticatie register), an organisation that enables the unique electronic identification of insurers and offices in healthcare. The logo creates a kind of pivot point with the vertices of the 'A' and 'V' characters.

☞ see Anatomy 26

A punctuation character used in many languages that use the Latin alphabet. It is used in the English language to indicate the omission of letters from a word, or the possessive case.

The apostrophe is also used in other languages to represent the omission of a sound in a word; to mark the point at which a word is divided into its root and its affixes; to represent palatisation (where certain vowels have an effect on nearby consonants) and to represent the glottal stop (the voiceless noise represented by the hyphen in the English word uh-oh).

The prime symbol (') is often confused with the apostrophe due to its similar appearance and the fact that many fonts offer one character for both purposes. However, a prime is a separate character that is used to designate various units, as well as mathematical and scientific expressions.

This is an apostrophe.

This is a prime.

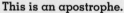

see Punctuation 207, Scientific characters 224

The act of acquiring something, often without the permission of the owner. Designers may appropriate typography from other designs, the built environment or antique books.

This poster was created by Why Not Associates for The Art of Lost Words exhibition at the text/gallery, London. Organisers asked 47 participants to contribute original work that used a forgotten word from the English language. This design appropriates a poster style from the early twentieth century.

An ancient Semitic language that is spoken throughout the Middle East and North Africa and the culture of its speakers. Arabic is read from right to left. Globalisation has given rise to Arabic being increasingly used in Western designs and conversely, English and other Latin-based languages being used in Arabic designs, as dual language designs become more common.

Arabic numerals were adopted in Europe in the Middle Ages and are now used in conjunction with the Latin alphabet. This system is based on the ten digits (0, 1, 2, 3, 4, 5, 6, 7, 8, 9) derived from the Hindu-Arabic that was developed by Indian mathematicians.

هي لغة سامية قديمة يتحدثها سكان منطقة الشرق الأوسط وشمال أفريقيا، وهي عبارة عن ثقافة الشعوب التي تتحدثها. اللغة العربية لغة تُقرأ من اليمين إلى اليسار. وقد أدت العولمة إلى تزايد استخدام اللغة العربية في التصاميم الغربية، كما أدت، على العكس من ذلك، إلى استخدام اللغة الإنجليزية واللغات الأخرى ذات الأصل اللاتيني في التصاميم العربية، حيث أصبحت التصاميم ثنائية اللغة أكثر انتشاراً.

تم استخدام الأرقام العربية في أوروبا في العصور الوسطى، وهي الآن تُستخدم جنباً إلى جنب مع الحروف الهجائية اللاتينية. ويستند هذا النظام إلى النظام المكون من عشرة أرقام (٠، ١، ٢، ٣، ٤، ٥، ٦، ٧، ٨، ٩) المشتقة من العربية الهندية والتي قام بتطويرها علماء الرياضيات الهنود.

☞ see Dual language 86, Non Latin 179

Type is frequently used in an architectural context, such as
inscriptions carved into stone or wood. The choice of font should
consider the visual impact of the shadows of the carved letters
and the scale they will be produced at. The lettering on
the lightwell of St Martin-in-the-Fields features a poem
by Andrew Motion, commissioned by Eric Parry
Architects. The lettering was designed by
Tom Perkins, and cast in polished stainless
steel in Eichenberger, Switzerland.

see Serif 226

A baseline is an imaginary line that all type characters sit upon. Some rounded characters, such as the 'o', actually fall slightly below the baseline. The location of the baseline varies for different typefaces as its position is fixed by a relative measurement. This information is embedded into the PostScript information that a font contains.

Text can be locked to the baseline (above) or unlocked, as it is here.

O

Note the letterform of the 'o' falling below the baseline.

Text can be aligned to a baseline, but text does not necessarily have to be set on each line of the baseline. Notice how this caption is set on each baseline but the body text is set on alternate baselines.

☞ see Alignment 22

A typographical tool that allows a designer to control
the repositioning of text away from the baseline of a
layout. Baseline shift can be used to position text above
or below the baseline as illustrated here.

Baseline	Higher	Lower
Type aligning to the baseline	Type aligning above the baseline	Type aligning below the baseline

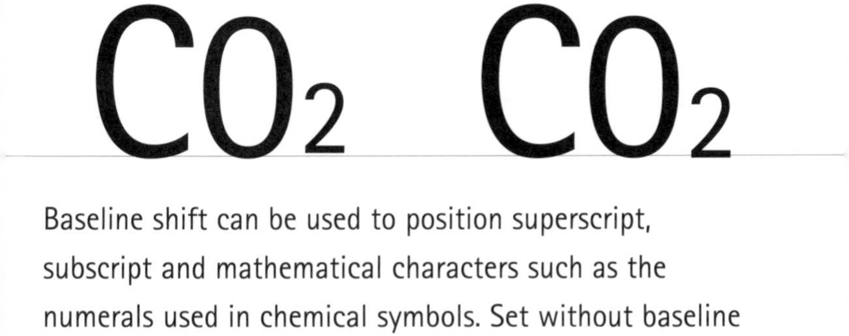

$$CO_2 \quad CO_2$$

Baseline shift can be used to position superscript,
subscript and mathematical characters such as the
numerals used in chemical symbols. Set without baseline
shift, the subscript 2 appears to float (left); it looks
better if aligned to the baseline (right).

☞ see Alignment 22

The printer and typographer (1706–1775) who sought to improve on the traditional typefaces by simplifying them and giving them more consistency in size and form. John Baskerville created his landmark transitional serif typeface, Baskerville, in 1757. Baskerville features increased stroke contrast, sharper and more tapered serifs, rounded letters with a more vertical axis and a more circular form to curves. These changes made the typeface more legible.

Baskerville was recut – and revived – in 1996, by Zuzana Licko for Emigre. This new version of the typeface was named Mrs Eaves, after Sarah Eaves, John Baskerville's wife and former housekeeper. She completed the printing of unfinished volumes that Baskerville left unfinished upon his death. The revised font contains a set of experimental ligatures, while retaining the characteristics of the original – compare the upper-case 'Q' for instance.

ABCDEFGHIJKLMNOPQRSTUVWXYZ
abcdefghijklmnopqrstuvwxyz1234567890

Baskerville, John Baskerville's original font

ABCDEFGHIJKLMNOPQRSTUVWXYZ
abcdefghijklmnopqrstuvwxyz1234567890
aefbctfyeeffgifhitfjkyflgggyoespggyfrstftip
pytwtttyttyffbffiffhffjckyfflffrfftffyfi

Mrs Eaves, a postmodern take on the original

☞ see Emigre 91, Ligatures 155, Postmodernism 199

the art and design school, bauhaus, opened in 1919, under
the direction of the renowned architect walter gropius.
the bauhaus aimed to provide a fresh approach to design
following the first world war. bauhaus designs are
characterised by economical and geometric forms
and typically sans serif fonts, and use the primary colours
and basic square, triangle and circle shapes.

pictured here is a bauhaus lithograph that features
sans serif text with even stroke weight.

see Reductionism 212

Type created for a specific client or usage. Bespoke typography is a driver for innovation and change in typography as designers seek differentiation and a graphic edge. Newspapers, magazines and consumer brands have long been users of bespoke type. For example, the typeface Times New Roman was created for the UK national daily newspaper *The Times* in 1931.

Shown here is the cover of *The Last Magazine*, a book by David Renard, created by Frost Design for Rizzolo International Publications. The book is based on the premise that magazines as we know them are a dying breed. The book assesses their future in relation to the emergence of the 'style press'; magazines that are physically and aesthetically engaging, as well as vibrant chroniclers of trends. The book features a bespoke font that symbolises the 'shredding' of magazines and their traditions.

A parametric curve that is used by computer vector graphics to model smooth curves that can be scaled. Bézier curves are used to form the curved paths of type. Bézier curves are also used to form the clipping paths of images obtained from image libraries. A clipping path is a series of points and paths drawn as Bézier curves that conform to the smooth and sharp points of the outline. An understanding and appreciation of letter shapes will help inform a designer's judgement when it comes to typographic choices and the subtle differences and intricacies of typefaces. Bézier curves were popularised by the French engineer, Pierre Bézier, who used them to design automobile bodies.

This letterform is constructed from a series of Bézier mathematical curves that allow it to be easily resized. In this sense, a font is constructed in the same way that a vector drawing file would be. This is why fonts can be reproduced at any size without loss of smoothness or quality.

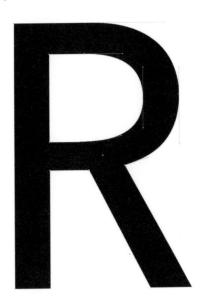

☞ see Vector 263

A letter constructed of a fixed number of pixels (or dots). The more frequent and finer the dots are, the sharper and more detailed the resulting character will be. Digital fonts used to be drawn at prescribed sizes, but now fonts 'recreate' themselves at any size by being constructed of a series of vectors, or mathematical formulae.

Most type management programs use 'anti-aliasing' to give a smooth appearance on screen. Grey pixels are applied to the edges, to prevent the stepped appearance of type, as illustrated below. A similar technique is used for coloured text, but instead of using grey pixels to smooth the type, lighter coloured pixels of the colour are used.

Without anti-aliasing

With anti-aliasing

☞ see Vector 263

A typeface based on the ornate writing style prevalent in Europe during the Middle Ages (fifth to sixteenth centuries). Also called Block, Gothic, Old English, Black or Broken, Black letter typefaces appear heavy and difficult to read in large text blocks due to their complex letterforms and the fact that they can seem antiquated and unfamiliar.

The quick brown fox jumps over the lazy dog

Engravers Old English

The quick brown fox jumps over the lazy dog

Black letter 686

An Italian engraver, publisher, printer and typographer (1740–1813) who created the typeface now known as Bodoni. As printer to the Duke of Parma, he oversaw the publication of many books, including the *Iliad* by Homer. Giambattista acquired a great technical ability that enabled him to reproduce thin hairlines, which could then be contrasted with thicker stroke weights on the character stems.

Bodoni is used in this invitation by Unthink for an exhibition by Peggy S. Guinness. Note the strong stroke contrast and delicate serifs.

☞ see Hairline 125, Serif 226

BODY COPY DOES NOT INCLUDE HEADLINES

OR SUBHEADS AND STANDFIRSTS

Body copy is the main text element of a publication or webpage and is also commonly referred to as a text block. Body copy is normally set in one or two columns that run down the

'PULL QUOTES ARE NOT CLASSED AS BODY COPY'

page although it can be set in more. Body copy is typically set with a type size ranging from nine to 12 points to make efficient use of the space available while still being large enough to be legible. Many typefaces have been developed specifically for body text and they tend to have characteristics (such as serifs) that make it easy for the eye to traverse across the page.

FOOTNOTES AND CAPTIONS ARE NOT BODY TEXT EITHER.

see Column 63, Text blocks 246

C G O Q

b d c e o p q

The part of a character that encloses a space in circular letterforms such as 'O' and 'e'. The bowl may be closed, as in the capital O, or open, as in a capital G.

Braces are used chiefly in mathematics, computing or textual notation.

They were once used horizontally to link displayed items in columns, but this has now been replaced by the rule.

Braces are used to enclose items of text that are to be considered...

...together.

☞ **see Brackets 46**

Typographical characters that provide different
ways of enclosing text.

( )

Parentheses, or open brackets, are round brackets used to enclose a
word or explanation inserted into a text passage.

[ ]

Square, closed or box brackets are used to enclose words added by
someone other than the original speaker or writer in a text passage.

{ }

Curly brackets, or braces, are used to enclose words
or text lines that are to be considered together.

Angle brackets, diamond brackets, cone brackets or chevrons are
used to enclose highlighted material such as short excerpts, to
denote dialogue that is thought instead of spoken, and to replace
the guillemets (« ») used as quotation marks in some languages,
when the proper glyphs are not available.

☞ see Brace 45, Glyphs 117, Punctuation 207

A reading and writing method for visually impaired people, which uses raised dots to represent letters and numbers. The braille system was created by Louis Braille in 1821. It uses a rectangular matrix of six dots that gives 64 possible combinations derived from the presence or absence of dots. Punctuation is represented by specific dot combinations.

Braille is included in signage design in many public places, such as lifts and information panels. It is also included in packaging design, particularly for pharmaceutical products.

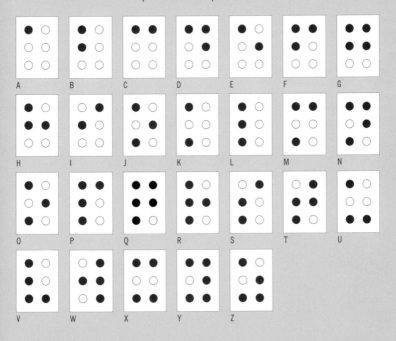

see Punctuation 207

A symbol, mark, word or phrase that identifies and differentiates a product, service or organisation from its competitors. Brands are created to help us distinguish between similar product offerings through perceptions of quality and value. The brand then becomes a recognisable symbol for a certain level of quality, which aids our buying decision. Brands often craft a 'personality', which represents a set of values that appeal to their target consumers; for example, foods are represented as 'healthier', or sauces 'tastier' than their competitors.

This identity, created by To The Point, uses a numeral as a letter to differentiate the brand.

☞ see Numerals 180

TEXT THAT HAS BEEN ROTATED 90 DEGREES TO THE
FORMAT OF A PUBLICATION. BROADSIDE TEXT IS USED TO
MAKE A VISUAL IMPRESSION OR TO PROVIDE A MORE
SUITABLE MEANS OF HANDLING TEXT ELEMENTS WITHIN
THE PUBLICATION'S FORMAT.

A graphic character, dot or mark that precedes items on a list. A bullet set in a list looks balanced when set next to a capital, but appears to float when the text is set minuscule. The position of a bullet can be adjusted using baseline shift to achieve a more balanced look.

- **A bullet aligned to the baseline can appear to float.**

- **A bullet with baseline shift applied can look more natural.**

Some fonts have bullets that are visually very different to the typeface that they accompany. Bullets may be relatively smaller or larger, while some fonts have circular bullets and others square or diamond shapes. Some varying sizes are shown below:

- **Wide Latin**   • Verdana

- Tiffany   • Onyx

☞ see Baseline shift 35, Minuscules 167

The art of fine handwriting. Calligraphy uses a pen with a nib or a brush to create characters that have different stroke widths, flourishes and other features that create a strong visual impression. Throughout the history of printing, fonts have been produced to replicate the attributes of handwritten characters, from Black letter to italics, as shown below.

ABCDEFGHIJKLMNOPQRSTUVWXYZ
abcdefghijklmnopqrstuvwxyz1234567890

Black letter 686 is a very ornate, traditional calligraphy-based typeface.

ABCDEFGHIJKLMNOPQRSTUVWXYZ
abcdefghijklmnopqrstuvwxyz1234567890

Sacre Bleu is a modern, more informal calligraphic typeface.

☛ see Black letter 41, Flourish 103, Italic 142

Cap height is the measurement from the baseline to the top of a capital letter. This measurement is made using a capital letter that is flat on top, and not a letter that has overshoot (for example an A or an O, that extend beyond and below). These characters overhang to make them look balanced compared to flatter characters. Without this overshoot, they'd look smaller.

Cap height

Height AO

Baseline

You'll notice that different typefaces have different cap heights when set at the same type size, as shown below.

H H H **H** **H**

It is also worth noticing that some cap heights vary in relation to x-heights. Fonts with large x-heights in relation to cap height are generally used for body copy as they remain legible at smaller type sizes.

Cap height

x-height

Hxk Hxk

Baseline

☞ see Baseline 34, X-height 271

THE USE OF CAPITAL LETTERS, OR MAJUSCULES, IN WRITING OR PRINTING. TYPE CAN BE SET IN ONE OF A NUMBER OF 'CASES':

UPPER CASE IS WHEN EACH LETTER IS A CAPITAL OR MAJUSCULE. SOME TYPEFACES, SUCH AS TRAJAN, ARE AVAILABLE IN UPPER CASE ONLY. LARGE AMOUNTS OF TEXT SET IN CAPITALS ARE CONSIDERED DIFFICULT TO READ.

lower case is when each letter is a small letter or minuscule. some typefaces, such as bayer, are available in lower case only.

<u>Title Case</u> Is When The First Letter Of Each Word In A Sentence Is A Capital.

<u>Sentence case</u> is when the first letter of the first word in a sentence only is a capital.

<u>InterCap</u> is where two words are joined, with a capital letter in the middle, and are common in logotypes, for example FedEx.

☞ see Majuscules 159, Minuscules 167, Word shape 270

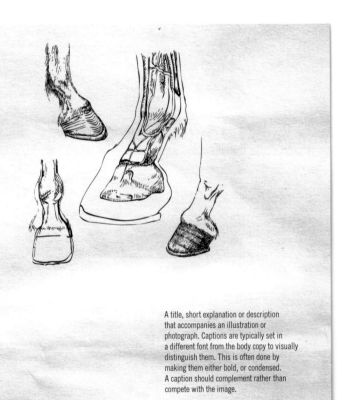

A title, short explanation or description
that accompanies an illustration or
photograph. Captions are typically set in
a different font from the body copy to visually
distinguish them. This is often done by
making them either bold, or condensed.
A caption should complement rather than
compete with the image.

☞ see Body copy 43, Condensed 67

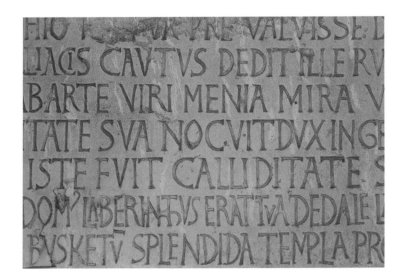

TO MAKE OR FORM LETTERS BY CUTTING INTO
STONE OR WOOD. THE ROMAN CIVILISATION
PRODUCED A GREAT NUMBER OF STONE
MONUMENTS ADORNED WITH CARVED TEXT.
THE LETTERS WERE CARVED TO BE READABLE AT
A DISTANCE AND USED THE SHADOWS CREATED
BY THE RECESSES TO CREATE VISUAL DEPTH.
THESE ANGULAR CARVINGS HAVE INSPIRED
MANY SUBSEQUENT TYPEFACES, SUCH AS
TRAJAN, USED HERE.

☞ see Architectural typography 33, Font/Typeface 106, Texture 250

English merchant, diplomat, writer and printer (c. 1415–1492) who introduced the printing press into England in 1476 and was the country's first printer. William Caxton printed most of his books in English and helped to standardise English language usage, formalise spelling and expand the English vocabulary. The introduction of printing and (later) moveable type allowed the mass publication of information and spread of learning. Type continues to benefit from technological change with computer technology and the Internet, making it easier and cheaper to create and disseminate information.

Pictured is a woodcut from Geoffrey Chaucer's *Canterbury Tales*, the first book that Caxton printed at his press in Westminster, London, in 1476.

Cinema uses the personality aspects of typefaces to help set the feel of a film in a way that the general public can easily grasp. Display and bespoke typefaces are typically used to create a specific visual identity for a film. Small amounts of text on posters and opening titles are set in large type sizes to draw maximum attention.

This typographic work for the poster (left) and titles (below) of the film *Public Enemies* was created by Research Studios. Notice how the type is kept to a minimum in order to focus attention on a concise message, which is supported by the type style – blocky sans serif characters in a steely monotone colour suggest a gritty subject matter.

see Personification 193

A nineteenth-century quest for an alternative
to italics to highlight text gave rise to this
sub-classification of slab serif typefaces.

Clarendon was registered in 1845 by Robert Besley
of the Fann Street Foundry, and variants were widely
used on Wild West 'Wanted' and 'Reward' posters.
It experienced a resurgence in the 1920s, when
newspaper production soared, and fonts that would
produce a good impression despite the wear of
industrial printing processes were required.

Clarendons have little stroke width variation and
relatively short serifs. There are three main variants:

ABCDEFGHIJKLMNOPQRSTUVWXYZ
abcdefghijklmnopqrstuvwxyz1234567890

Clarendon (19th Century): typeface shown is Cheltenham. Clarendon fonts have small arcs that bracket the serifs.

ABCDEFGHIJKLMNOPQRSTUVWXYZ
abcdefghijklmnopqrstuvwxyz1234567890

Clarendon (Neo): typeface shown is Century Schoolbook. Clarendon Neo fonts have greater stroke weight contrast.

ABCDEFGHIJKLMNOPQRSTUVWXYZ
abcdefghijklmnopqrstuvwxyz1234567890

Clarendon (Legibility): typeface shown is Ionic. Clarendon Legibility fonts have a larger x-height and were created for use on low-grade papers.

☞ see X-height 271

Various systems that seek to instill a meaningful order to the plethora of typefaces that exist. Classification systems allow a designer to make more informed typographical decisions and to obtain a better understanding of type. There is no straightforward, standard-type classification system as several systems exist, with varying degrees of complexity. Typefaces can be classified according to their inherent characteristics, the time period in which they were developed, or their typical usage. A simple classification could be, for example: serif, sans serif and decorative.

Serif – for example Garamond

Sans Serif – for example Univers

Slab Serif – for example Memphis

Script – for example Santa Fe

Decorative – for example Jazz

Modern – for example Bodoni

Geometric – for example Avante Garde

Humanist – for example Sabon

Transitional – for example Baskerville

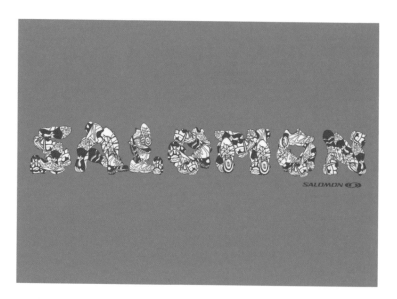

Fabric and materials that cover the body. Clothing serves a number of functions; from providing protection and warmth, to projecting self-image and a sense of style or fashion. In consumer cultures, typography plays an important role in clothing due to the branding, logos and slogans that garments often carry.

The design above by Studio Output for sports clothing brand Salomon, features the brand name in a bespoke type made from shoe images.

☛ see T-Shirt 256

A group of different fonts for use in a particular publication or design. A designer selects a collection of fonts with which to create a typographical hierarchy for a given design or publication. It is necessary to consider how the different fonts will interact with and complement each other on the page.

For example

You may need a typeface for headlines, this could be a bold sans serif, and then a typeface for body copy, in this example a serif book face.*

* you may also need a typeface for captions, and this could, for example, be a lighter and smaller version of the headline font, creating a degree of symbiosis and hierarchy.

If typefaces are too similar

In this instance Bookman has been used for the headline, and Garamond for the body copy. As they are similar it would be better to use only one font, at a different size, to establish the hierarchy.

Equally, if they are too different

They will appear as though they have no natural relationship. Finding the correct balance for type collections takes time and patience, but as a general rule they shouldn't be too similar, or too different.

☞ see Font/Typeface 106, Hierarchy 130

In typography, it is the density of the textual coverage on a page that effectively 'colours' it. A designer can use typographic colour to create contrast and tension in a design, particularly when there is also a great deal of white space. A designer needs to consider how typographic colour will affect a design, so as to prevent unwanted results. The amount of typographic colour present in a design is a factor of the quantity of text and how it is set.

Each typeface provides differing amounts of colouration due to differences in stroke width, x-height, character width, serif style and other decorative elements. Leading, tracking, letter spacing and kerning are all typographic tools that can be used to increase or reduce the colour density of a text block. This text is printed in two different fonts to illustrate the point. Univers 75 Bold (top) and Rotis Sans Serif light (bottom) clearly produce different levels of typographic colour.

☞ see Serif 226, X-height 271

Headlines and straplines are often formed from a few words that span the entire column width or several columns to create impact.

Text is flowed into columns so that it is presented in an organised manner. Columns give a strong sense of order to a design but can also make it overly static if there is little text variation or few opportunities to vary text block presentation. Varying column widths to produce an asymmetrical appearance adds dynamism and interest to a design.

Columns for supporting text such as marginalia are often narrower than the main text columns. Using the combination of type size and leading, marginalia text can be made to cross align with the body text.

$$2\,|000$$

$$15\,|150$$

A punctuation mark used to indicate a separation of ideas or of elements within the structure of a sentence. In typography, a comma is also used in the presentation of large numbers, such as those pictured. Within this context, tabbing can be used to align the numbers on the comma to make the figures easier to read. As the commas in the above example align, the digits no longer do so because the number 1 occupies less space than the other numbers. In instances where alignment is important, such as financial results, it may be necessary to use monospaced fonts for numerals.

☞ see Numerals 180, Punctuation 207

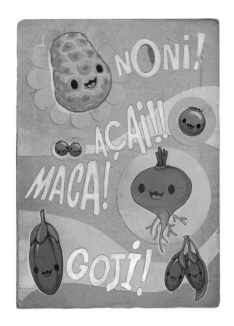

Being contracted, hired or awarded a job to create a specific product or service. As with all commissions, you need to be clear what you are delivering, and what you will be paid in return. It will also be necessary to have contracts in place for larger commissions to protect both parties.

Pictured above is an illustration by Richard Wilkinson, commissioned by the UK's *Telegraph magazine* to accompany a feature about the health benefits of certain so-called superfoods. Different plants are depicted as cartoon characters, shouting their own names out in hand-drawn text.

Multiple typefaces used together harmoniously in a design; complementary fonts are used when the use of a single font may not produce a workable result. Complementary fonts can add different levels of texture and nuance to a design. A hierarchy can also be introduced to different levels of text in this way.

Alternatively, different fonts that would not normally be used together can be mixed up to make a graphic statement. This brochure, created by To The Point Design Studio, draws interest to a page of statistics by using complementary fonts at different point sizes and orientations.

☞ see Orientation 186, Point size 196

A narrower version of a typeface than the roman cut. Condensed types are useful for situations where space is tight (for example newspapers) and they provide designers with typesetting flexibility while remaining within the same font family. As not all fonts have an accompanying condensed version you'll need to forward plan.

Grotesque
Grotesque Condensed

News Gothic
News Gothic Condensed

Futura
Futura Condensed

Eurostile
Eurostile Condensed

Garamond Book
Garamond Book Condensed

☞ see Face/Family 97

A process whereby a design is built rather than crafted. The
iteration of an idea, developed and constructed by sequential
steps, to meet a design brief. Pictured is type created by 3 Deep
Design as part of an identity for Australian paper distributor,
Raleigh Paper, to promote Nordset – an environmentally
responsible, chlorine-free paper. The letters appear as a sheet
of paper passing through an offset printing machine.

☞ see Craft 73, Font/Typeface 106

A modern art movement that originated in Russia in the early 1920s. Constructivism is characterised by the use of industrial materials, such as glass, sheet metal and plastic, to create non-representational, often geometric objects. It also involved a wide-ranging commitment to total abstraction. Russian constructivism was highly influential on modernism through its use of black and red sans serif typography, often arranged in asymmetrical blocks. Leading constructivist practitioners include Wassily Kandinsky, Alexander Rodchenko and El Lissitzky. Shown here is the title page from El Lissitzky's *Victory Over the Sun* series.

The opposition of elements to emphasise the differences between them. Contrast is a key visual device that enables a design to highlight and draw attention to specific information. Contrast is often provided through the use of high-contrast colour combinations, such as yellow and black (also found in natural forms); but it can also be created through scale (large and small), substrate (smooth versus rough finishes), finishing (UV varnish), or other attributes.

This identity, created by Pentagram for the Villeroy & Boch brand, Vivo, features black text that contrasts with the white china it is set against. The scale of the text also creates contrast with the size of the object. In this instance, the Vivo identity hints at a sense of care and craft, while the trade name below the logotype gives a sense of heritage and quality. Note that the text presents a hierarchy of information, concluding with the place of manufacture.

☞ see Bespoke typography 38, Identity 136, Logotype 157, Scale 223

Typography that reflects the values of a corporation.
Corporate typography does not have to be conservative or
boring. Choosing type to establish a corporate identity can be
quite challenging and often results in avante-garde creations like
this example, created by 3 Deep Design for the State Library
of Victoria, Australia. The typography gives the organisation
a unique and distinct image.

☞ see Branding 48, Commission 65, Identity 136, Logotype 157

The empty space inside the body stroke of a character. Counters are seen in minuscule (lower case) a, b, d, e, g, o, p and q characters, as well as in many of their majuscule (upper case) counterparts.

Pictured is a design by Holly Wales, where the counters have been intentionally removed.

☞ see Bowl 44, Majuscules 159, Minuscules 167

Proficiency in doing or making something. In design terms, craft is the use of the designer's skill to fashion something exquisite and precise. Design craft can be seen in the production of detailed engravings or filigree, the screen-printing of complex multi-coloured images, and the drafting of new fonts, such as in this book cover by Andy Vella. The layering of hand-drawn typography and subtle overprinting creates a rich tapestry of type and image.

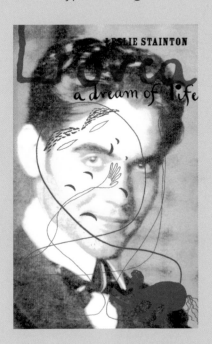

Copyright Andy Vella

☞ see Hand drawn 126, Overprinting 190, Weight 268

A heading set in body text to break it into easily readable sections. Cross heads can be set in a different font, point size or colour in order to create a more visually arresting break, as shown below.

Simple form

At its simplest, a cross head is set in the same type size and colour as the body text and is perhaps distinguished by the use of additional spacing.

More contrast

To further distinguish a cross head, it can be emboldened to create an obvious information hierarchy.

Alternatively

Use of different fonts and colours and tints increases the distinction between cross heads and text.

CAPS

Distinction can also be achieved by setting cross heads in capitals.

Effective cross heads generally use a consistent format and can be achieved without needing to change colour, size, typeface or position in order to create difference. Less is often more.

☞ see Contrast 70, Hierarchy 130

Beatrice Ward delivered a speech to the British Typographers' Guild in 1932 called *The Crystal Goblet*, or *Printing Should Be Invisible*, an extract of which is printed below.

'You have two goblets before you. One is of solid gold, wrought in the most exquisite patterns. The other is of crystal-clear glass, thin as a bubble, and as transparent. Pour and drink; and according to your choice of goblet, I shall know whether or not you are a connoisseur of wine. For if you have no feelings about wine one way or the other, you will want the sensation of drinking the stuff out of a vessel that may have cost thousands of pounds; but if you are a member of that vanishing tribe, the amateurs of fine vintages, you will choose the crystal, because everything about it is calculated to reveal rather than hide the beautiful thing which it was meant to contain.'

This essay is of fundamental importance to typography, and for many students it represents their first encounter with the idea of *talking* and *thinking* about type design. The essay uses the wine glass as a metaphor and questions whether the wine would taste better if served in a clear crystal glass or an ornate goblet. The point of the analogy is that typographic design is also a container; should it be an elaborate one that obscures the content or a transparent one that allows it to shine through? *The Crystal Goblet* shifted the focus away from 'How should it look?' towards modern values of 'What must it do?', which is the typographical interpretation of 'form follows function'.

Various special typographical characters or symbols that graphically represent the unit of different currencies. Currency symbols are relatively rare, in that few currencies have a specific symbol. The lines through a currency symbol represent stability. Countries that do not have a currency symbol typically use an abbreviation of the currency unit name, such as COP for Colombian pesos or CLP for Chilean pesos.

Pound
The symbol for pound sterling used in the UK. The symbol evolved from an L, for 'librum', Latin for weight.

Dollar
The symbol for the US and Australian dollar and also a wide range of Latin American currencies.

Euro
The symbol for the Euro, the currency of the European Union.

Yen
The symbol for the Japanese yen.

Cent
The symbol for the US cent, a subdivision of the dollar.

Dong
The symbol for the Vietnamese dong.

see Comma 64, Numerals 180

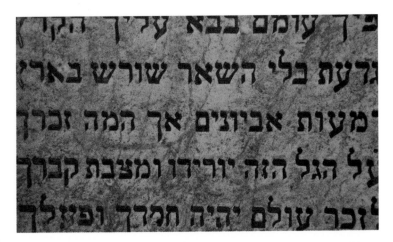

Alphabets based on Glagolitic, an alphabet developed by missionaries during the ninth century to translate the Bible for the Great Moravia region. Cyrillic alphabets are used for Slavic languages, such as Russian. The current Cyrillic alphabet was adopted in 1708 during the reign of Peter the Great of Russia, with a further modification in 1917/18 when four letters were eliminated. The Cyrillic alphabet is the basis of over 50 different languages in Russia, Central Asia and Eastern Europe. Many of these use additional characters that have been adapted from standard Cyrillic letters, and others taken from the Greek or Latin alphabets.

The script shown here is carved on to a gravestone in a Jewish cemetery in Warsaw, Poland.

☞ see Alphabet 23

DUTCH FOR 'THE STYLE', AN ART AND DESIGN MOVEMENT THAT DEVELOPED AROUND A MAGAZINE OF THE SAME NAME FOUNDED BY THEO VAN DOESBURG. DE STIJL USED STRONG RECTANGULAR FORMS, EMPLOYED PRIMARY COLOURS AND CELEBRATED ASYMMETRICAL COMPOSITIONS. PICTURED IS A LITHOGRAPH POSTER CREATED BY THEO VAN DOESBURG AND VILMOS HUSZAR IN 1917. IT FEATURES TYPOGRAPHY WITH THE CHARACTERISTIC RECTANGULAR FORMS.

The literal and primary meaning of an image, graphic or text. The **denotive** meaning of a piece of text is what it literally means: nothing more, nothing less. **Cognition** is understanding, knowing or interpreting, based on what has been perceived, learned or reasoned. The cognitive interpretation of text depends upon how it is presented.

Pictured here is a book cover created by Andy Vella. Notice that the lack of a counter in the 'o' of extinction provides a cognitive meaning that reinforces the subject matter.

see Counter 72

A unit of typographical measurement, based on a system created by Pierre Fournier. In Fournier's system, an approximate French inch is divided by 12 to calculate one ligne, which is then divided by six to get one point. Didot adapted this system to make the base unit (one French inch) identical to the standard value defined by the government. The Didot point has been widely used in European countries and one point is equal to 0.376mm.

An American point system has also been developed, using units called picas (one pica = 4.233mm).

Fournier's original method has been restored in today's digital typography.

Shown below is Fournier's scale of his point system, from *Manuel Typographique*, Barbou, Paris 1764.

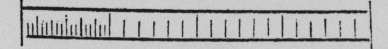

É CHELLE FIXE
de 144 points Typographiques.

see Em and en 89, Point size 196

A print-finishing process whereby part of the substrate is cut away using a steel die. Mainly used for decorative purposes, a die cut can be used to enhance the visual impact of type within a design. When die cutting type it is important to consider what will be removed; the counters of certain letters, for example. Pictured is a magazine cover created by Frost Design for Trio, a property complex in Sydney, Australia. The logo uses vertical die-cut strokes to draw parallels with the vertical structure of the buildings within the complex.

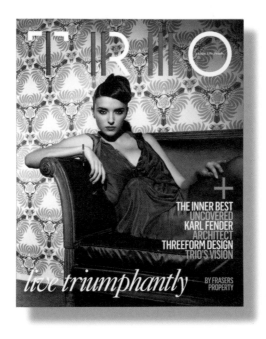

☞ see Print finishing 201

Fonts created digitally rather than by hand. The digital revolution has meant that new fonts can be designed and trialled quickly and easily, without the great time and expense of producing hot metal type. With the emergence of digital type foundries such as Bitstream and T·26, the production of digital fonts further separated type design from type manufacturers. The explosive growth in the processing power of personal computers and the increasing performance of software has made typeface design more straightforward, allowing designers to produce bespoke type, such as this from 3 Deep Design, more easily.

☞ **see Bezier 39, Vector 263**

Zapf Dingbats

Wingdings

Webdings

Cable Dingbats

An ornamental typographic character. Dingbats are symbols, such as arrows, stars and ticks, that are used for emphasis in display. At first glance, dingbats or printers' ornaments may appear to be somewhat gimmicky, but they offer a varied and flexible set of extra characters that can be helpful additions when typesetting. Various different sets of dingbats are available, such as those shown here. Dingbats are not to be confused with other special typographical symbols, such as pi characters and fleurons.

☞ see Fleurons 102, Pi characters 194

DISPLAY FACES, OFTEN CALLED ORNAMENTAL TYPE, ARE TYPEFACES DESIGNED FOR USE AT LARGER SIZES ONLY. THIS FONT, GLASER STENCIL, WAS DESIGNED BY MILTON GLASER IN 1970 AND IS AN UNICASE (OMNICASE) FONT, CONTAINING NO LOWERCASE CHARACTERS.

Display faces are often used as headline copy, or in posters and large displays. This font by Otto Eckmann, an active 'floral' Jugendstilist, would clearly not be appropriate for body copy or long passages of text.

Display fonts often have accompanying variations, which are less exaggerated. For example, this is an extended and emboldened version of Univers, a font available in variants that are suitable for longer passages of text.

These fonts can also be called poster, as the example here, Bodoni Poster, demonstrates.

n enlarged capital letter at the start of a paragraph that drops down a specified number of lines into it. The height of a drop cap is determined by the number of text lines it extends over. This is typically three, but it varies depending on the font and how elaborate the drop cap is. Drop caps can be very ornate, highly decorated and coloured, or simply an enlarged letter of the font a text is set in. Drop caps create a strong visual entrance to a piece of text, although certain letter shapes are more conducive to creating a strong visual hook than others. For example, letters with square shapes such as 'H' tend to work better than curved letters that bend away from the text block, as these can create an awkward-looking space.

rop caps are distinct from Standing Capitals, which are enlarged initial capitals that sit on the baseline of a text, creating a strong visual entry point due to the white space that surrounds them.

🖝 **see Baseline 34**

The presentation of text in two languages. Dual-language publications present information so that it can be read and understood by people from two or more different language groups. Dual-language publications are commonly found in locations where there may be many foreign tourists, at events celebrated by organisations from different nations and in government communications. The use of dual languages presents specific challenges for a designer, as the text for any given phrase will occupy different amounts of space when rendered in each language.

Pictured is a design by Wordsearch for the architectural firm, JRA, which uses both English and Arabic to convey the main selling points for the residential developments featured.

☞ see Arabic 32

TYPOGRAPHY THAT IS COMPOSED OF ELEMENTS DRAWN FROM VARIOUS SOURCES, SYSTEMS OR STYLES. DERIVING FROM THE GREEK *EKLEKTIKOS*, MEANING TO SELECT, ECLECTIC DESCRIBES THE USE OF SEVERAL INDIVIDUAL ELEMENTS.

THESE POSTERS COMBINE TYPEFACES AND FOUND OBJECTS TO PRODUCE A VISUALLY ARRESTING DESIGN. CREATED BY RESEARCH STUDIOS FOR THE MODA FAD FASHION EVENT IN BARCELONA, SPAIN, THEY FEATURE TEXT AS A GRAPHIC ELEMENT LAYERED OVER THE ARTWORK.

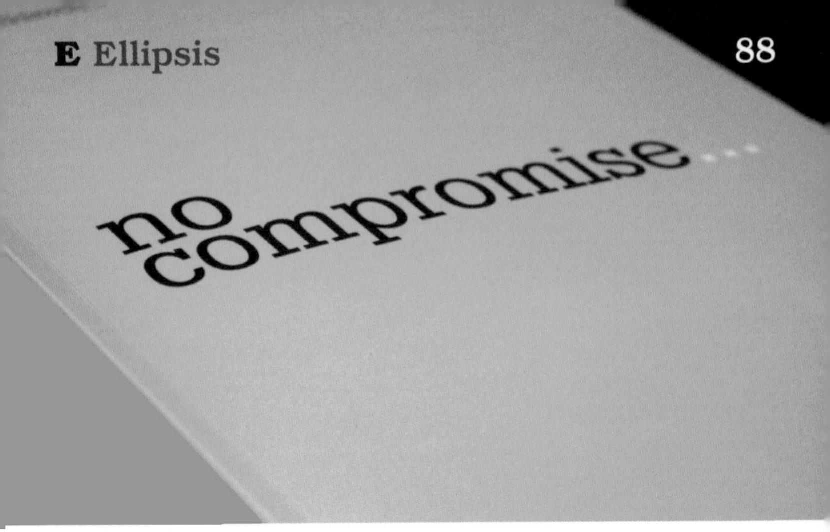

no compromise...

A punctuation mark formed by a series of three periods or dots. Used in text to indicate an omission or incomplete statement. Used at the end of a sentence, the ellipsis is followed by a full stop that is sometimes called a four-point ellipsis (as shown below). A true ellipsis has specific spacing that differs from a generated ellipsis and as it is a single unit, it will not split like the generated version. The dots may be square or round depending upon the font.

This book cover by To The Point features an ellipsis, designed to entice the reader to turn the cover....

● ● ●

Generated ellipsis, made of three periods, or full stops

● ● ●

True ellipsis, made of a single unit or glyph, note the difference in spacing

☞ see Punctuation 207

Typographical units of relative measurement. An em is
a unit of measurement derived from the width of the
square body of the metal cast majuscule 'M', and equals
the size of a given type. For example, 10pt type has a
10pt em. An en is half of an em. Neither ems nor ens
have anything to do with the size of the 'M' or 'N'
characters, which occupy different amounts of the em
square depending upon the characteristics of the font.

Pictured here are three em squares of the same point
size, each containing an M character. Notice how
although each M character has the same point size,
they each occupy a different amount of space
within the em square.

Hoefler Text   Italian Old Style   ITC Century

☞ see Majuscules 159

The process of stamping text or images into a substrate to give a raised surface (emboss) or recessed surface (deboss). Embossing and debossing can use ink or foil to colour or pattern the design. Where ink or foil is not used, it is a blind emboss or deboss (as in the example, above, by February London). To emboss and deboss text the type needs to be of sufficient point size and weight to give a good impression and in order for detail not to be lost.

☞ see Foil 104, Print finishing 201

An independent digital type foundry, founded by Rudy VanderLans and Zuzana Licko in Berkeley, California. Emigre helped pioneer digital typeface design in the 1980s and 1990s, producing typefaces that harnessed the possibilities of digital methods, rather than replicating letterpress methods. The company also published Emigre magazine between 1984 and 2005 to showcase many of its designs.

This text is set in one of Emigre's best-known typefaces, Citizen.

☞ see Baskerville, John 36, Digital fonts 82

A sequence of ordinary type characters used to express emotions in electronic communications such as email, chat and texting. Emoticons, or smileys, enable the senders to add feeling to a text communication and indicate how the recipient should interpret it. The meaning of short bursts of text can be taken in the wrong way but smileys are used to indicate that a phrase should not be taken too seriously.

:-)	Smiling, happy	**:D**	Large grin or laugh	**:O**	Shocked or surprised
:-(	Frowning, sad	**:-p**	Tongue out or, after a joke, I'm an idiot	**:-**	Bored, annoyed or awkward, concerned
;-)	Wink	**:>**	Love	**:-s**	Confused, embarrassed or uneasy
8-)	Cool, wearing sunglasses	**:-X**	Kissing	**:-()**	Yelling

Type set in the physical environment. Type surrounds us in the built environment, through its use in signage in public buildings, offices, galleries and as street signs. To be effective, type must be both of sufficient size and legible enough to be read at a reasonable viewing distance. The example shown, by Studio Myerscough for Vitra, demonstrates the impact of typography in an environmental space.

Various collectable items that designers use for reference and inspiration
for type design. Ephemera may include tickets, posters, postcards,
magazines and found objects. Ephemera provide a means of revisiting the
typefaces used in the past, which designers may then update for use in
contemporary designs.

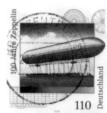

A system of moral principles and/or rules of conduct that centre on the difference between 'right' and 'wrong'. Ethics in design involves issues about what text and image content may be acceptable to wider society. Many countries seek to regulate content and protect the public through laws; designers in turn often push the limits of ethical acceptability, as notions of where these parameters lie are constantly changing. For example, it is now common to see nudity in fairly mainstream publications; while in the past, this was prohibited for ethical reasons – such as to preserve a sense of 'common decency'.

Ethics also inform the choices made by a design practice at a corporate level, such as the type of companies it will or will not work with, and the materials it uses, such as paper from sustainable forests and vegetable-based printing inks.

Pictured above is the Let's Be Honest T-shirt, designed by Ken Meier and David Yun for 'Part of It', a charity-driven project that invited designers and artists to create an image about a cause they feel passionate about. This T-shirt benefits the Free Press, a US-based, non-partisan organisation working to reform American media by promoting transparency and trust, the cornerstones of a responsible and accountable media.

An extended set of special characters that accompany a particular typeface. Expert sets include a range of characters that are not part of the usual typeface set, such as ligatures, fractions, small capitals, the dotless 'i' and lining numerals. The addition of an expert set gives a designer greater control over text presentation and helps solve some of the common typographical problems that standard character sets present.

Not all typefaces have an accompanying expert set, which means a designer needs to anticipate whether the design will need such characters when choosing the typefaces for a design.

Qwerty 1234567890

Garamond with lining numerals

QWERTY 1234567890

Garamond Expert with small caps and Old-Style numerals

ffi fl ffl

Ligature characters

⅔ ⅜ ⅝ ⅜ ⅞

Fraction characters

☞ see Fractions 110, Small capitals 235

All the variations of a particular typeface or font including all the different weights, widths and italics. Many families are named after their creator or the publication in which they were first used. Type families offer a designer a set of variations that work together in a clean and consistent way and, as such, are a useful design tool. To achieve clarity and a uniform feel to a piece of work, many designers restrict themselves to using only two type families for a project, meeting their requirements from the type variations these contain to establish the typographic hierarchy. Some type families cross many typographical boundaries; for example, a font may be available as a serif, a sans serif and even a semi serif, as shown below.

Rotis Serif
Rotis Sans Serif
Rotis Semi Sans
Rotis Semi Serif

☞ see Classification systems 59, Font libraries 107

'Fat Face' typefaces are a development from Modern typefaces. Used primarily in advertising and titling, these faces appeared from around 1810–1820. Elephant, Bodoni Ultra and Normande (shown here) are all examples.

They exaggerated the contrast of Modern typefaces, with slab-like verticals and more emphasis on vertical serifs, which often terminated in a wedge shape.

see Modern 169, Serif 226, Titling typefaces 252

A numerical series in which each number is the sum of the preceding two numbers in the sequence. Fibonacci numbers are named after the mathematician Fibonacci, or Leonardo of Piso, who observed this sequence in the proportions of the natural world. Numbers from the Fibonacci sequence are used in art, architecture and design as they provide a ready source of dimensions that produce harmonious proportions. The number sequence is shown below.

0, 1, 1, 2, 3, 5, 8, 13, 21, 34, 55, 89, 144...

Fibonacci numbers can be used to divide a page into areas with harmonious proportions and to establish relationships between typography and spacing, as the hierarchy below shows.

Headlines set at 34 point

With body copy set at 13 point

And image captions set at 8 point

A decorative typographical device or symbol used for
pointing at or highlighting a certain element of a piece of
text or image, such as the footnotes in this book. Also
called a printer's hand.

Monospaced, or fixed-width type aligns each character vertically by allocating the same amount of space to each one, whether it be a wide character such as a 'w', a narrow character such as an 'i', or a punctuation mark. Fixed-width fonts have numerals that vertically align, which makes them useful where numerical information needs to be set as financial data.

Notice how the following numerals align with text:
123456789

Fleurons are ornamental characters based on
the shapes of flowers, leaves and other floral
motifs. They are used for decorative purposes,
such as borders and breaks to separate
different content. Fleurons are not to be
confused with other special typographical
symbols, such as pi characters or dingbats.

☞ see Dingbats 83, Pi characters 194

A swash or curved, swirled line or tail that is used to enhance the appearance of a letter. A flourish increases the visual presence of a character, which is why they are sometimes used on drop caps at the start of text blocks.

☞ see Drop caps 85, Swash 245

A print-finishing material stamped on to a substrate using a heated die. This technique is also called foil block, block print or hot foil stamp. Foils typically come in metallic tones, such as gold, silver and copper, although other colours such as metallic blue, green and red are available. This piece, created by Gavin Ambrose for Project Perfection, features silver foil-blocked text.

☞ see Die cut 81, Print finishing 201

Folios refer to the sequential numbers on the pages of a publication. Folios can be positioned in various places to be more or less noticeable, calm or active. Folios are normally positioned in the top or bottom margin where they are passive, but they can also be positioned in the fore-edge margin where they are more active.

Preliminary pages are often numbered using Roman numerals as shown below:

I	1	XVIII	18	XCIX	99
II	2	XIX	19	C	100
III	3	XX	20	CL	150
IV	4	XXI	21	CC	200
V	5	XXV	25	CCC	300
VI	6	XXX	30	CD	400
VII	7	XXXV	35	CDXCIX	499
VIII	8	XL	40	D	500
IX	9	XLV	45	DC	600
X	10	XLIX	49	DCLXVI	666
XI	11	L	50	DCC	700
XII	12	LX	60	DCCC	800
XIII	13	LXIX	69	CM	900
XIV	14	LXX	70	CMXCIX	999
XV	15	LXXVI	76	M	1,000
XVI	16	LXXX	80		
XVII	17	XC	90		

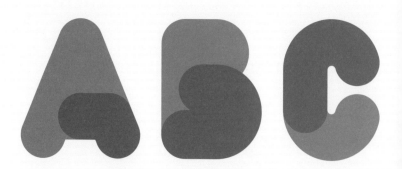

ABCDEFGHIJKLMNOPQRSTUVWXYZ
ABCDEFGHIJKLMNOPQRSTUVWXYZ
ABCDEFGHIJKLMNOPQRSTUVWXYZ

The letters, numbers and punctuation marks of a type design.
In common usage, the words 'typeface' and 'font' are used
synonymously; however, each term possesses a separate and distinct
meaning. A typeface is a collection of characters with the
same distinct design; while a font is the physical means of typeface
production – be it lithographic film, metal, or the description of a
typeface in computer code.

Pictured are three different weights of the typeface Aniboom, created
by Research Studios for an animation-sharing website, similar in
concept to YouTube.

☞ see Punctuation 207, Weight 268

Most font libraries are now online, where typefaces can be viewed prior to purchasing via a download. To a certain extent these have replaced specimen books, and have the advantage of offering immediate purchase and download.

Most libraries, like the Linotype example shown below, have sophisticated databases, collating fonts into many different categories, which can help with searching. They also nearly all allow a user to trial sample setting of text, in different sizes, weights and colours.

Fonts are often a lot more economical to buy than people realise, and this exposes you to a much wider range of possibilities and choices, rather than relying on old favourites.

☞ see Classification systems 59, Face/Family 97

Text positioned within the bottom margin of a page and usually repeated throughout a document. The footer typically includes information such as a title, date or page number. This brochure by February Design features a footer that is placed off-centre to add a touch of dynamism to the design.

☞ see Folio 105, Header/Running head 129

Notes that are referred to within the body text[†]

[†] and placed at the foot of the page. Footnotes are usually set in a smaller point size than the body text and are referred to by numerals, letters or a series of typographic symbols, such as asterisks (*), daggers (†), double daggers (††) and so on.

There are different conventions for the order that these symbols appear, but one example would be: *, †, ‡, §, ||, #, **, ††. If more symbols are needed, you simply have to triple or quadruple to continue the sequence.

Characters that represent parts of whole numbers. Fractions can be represented typographically in two ways: as en (or nut) fractions with a horizontal bar, or em fractions with a diagonal bar. Diagonal fractions are more pleasing to the eye and are commonly included with expert sets. These are also called em fractions as the bar is an em in length. Nut fractions, or horizontal fractions, are less common and have a bar that is an en in length. Most fonts have a fraction bar so designers can construct their own fractions. A fraction bar is a kerned character, so will not push the numerals away a full em space. When building fractions, character weight is lighter so they should be built in a medium weight to match a regular font.

Level fractions

Fraction bar

Nut fractions

1 / 2

¹/₂

1
―
2

Fractions with a diagonal bar one em in length and full-size numerals

The bar that separates the numerator and denominator figures of the fraction

Fractions with a horizontal bar one en in length

see Baseline shift 35, Em and en 89, Kerning 149, Numerals 180

A sub-group of Black letter typefaces. Fraktur fonts include the 26 letters of the Latin alphabet, plus an additional three vowels with umlauts: Ä, Ö, Ü, ä, ö and ü. Fraktur derives from the Latin past participle 'fractus', meaning 'broken'. Fraktur was created by Hieronymus Andreae during the reign of Holy Roman Emperor Maximilian I (1459–1519) for a series of books he commissioned. Some examples are shown below:

Textur	Rotunda	Schwabacher	Fraktur
a	a	a	a
d	d	d	d
g	g	g	g
n	n	n	n
o	o	o	o
A	A	A	A
B	B	B	B
H	H	S	H
S	S	S	S

☞ see Black letter 41, Latin typefaces 146

A typeface numbering system created by Adrian Frutiger for the Univers family, in order to identify the width and weight of each of the family's 21 original cuts. The numbering system was designed to eliminate the confusion caused by different naming systems.

The diagrammatic presentation of the Univers family brings a sense of order and homogeneity to the typeface's varying inter-relationships of weight and width. The grid is a modernist structure and uses numbers to identify the different cuts. The grid is intended to make type selection simpler and ultimately more useful, although it may appear complicated at first glance. The italic version of a font, *56*, can be used seamlessly with its roman, 55, for example. Varying character weight is easily achieved by moving one row down the grid from 55 to **65**, or if a bold is required, down to **75** if 55 and **65** are too similar in character weight.

The main numbers in Helvetica for example are 55 for roman, **75** for bold, 35 for thin and 25 for light, while many other numbers are not commonly used. For example, *68* is still called medium condensed oblique. While this grid system may initially be daunting and quite complex to the novice, its inherent logical organisation means that it can be understood and used as a productive design tool within a short space of time.

This page is set in Helvetica, one of many fonts that use this system. Others include Univers, Glypha and Frutiger.

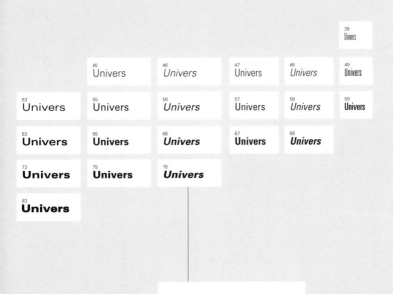

76
Univers

In any number from Frutiger's grid, the first digit, or designator, refers to the line weight. The thinnest is 2, with line weight incrementally getting fuller up to 9, its widest. The second digit refers to the character width, with 3 being the most extended and 9 the most condensed. Finally, even numbers indicate an italic face and odd numbers represent a roman face.

☞ see Face/Family 97, Modernism 170, Naming 177, Weight 268

● cdeo

Sans serif typefaces that are based on geometric shapes. Geometric typefaces tend to be rounded and typically have spacious capitals and numerals, with full circles for the 'O', 'Q', 'G' and 'C' letters. Angular characters, such as 'M', 'N', 'V' and 'W' are distinguishable by their splayed legs and arms. The development of geometric typefaces was inspired by constructivism, a modern art movement originating in Moscow in 1920 that favoured the use of geometric forms. This was built upon by the 1920s German Bauhaus movement, whose geometric shapes were made with a compass and T-square.

This text is set in Kabel. Art deco elements such as the seemingly awkward angles of some of the curves make Kabel appear very different from other geometric modernist typefaces.

ABCDEFGHIJKLMNOPQRSTUVWXYZ
abcdefghijklmnopqrstuvwxyz1234567890

Futura was designed by Paul Renner in 1927 and is considered the major typeface development to come out of the constructivist orientation of the Bauhaus movement. Typographer Paul Renner based the characters on the simple forms of circle, triangle and square, but softened them to be more legible and to create a new, modern type that was more than a revival.The long elegant ascenders and descenders benefit from generous line spacing and help create this striking and radical typeface.

British sculptor, typographer, stonecutter and printmaker (1882–1940). Taught by Edward Johnston, who designed the London Underground signage, Eric Gill created the humanist sans serif Gill Sans typeface family in the 1920s. Gill Sans has more classical proportions than Johnston's typeface design and includes a flared capital R and eyeglass lower-case g and geometric touches.

Johnston's Underground

ABCDEFGHIJKLMNOPQRSTUVWXYZ
abcdefghijklmnopqrstuvwxyzl234567890

Gill Sans

ABCDEFGHIJKLMNOPQRSTUVWXYZ
abcdefghijklmnopqrstuvwxyz1234567890

Notice how Gill Sans has circular dots above the i and j where Underground has diamond-shaped dots. Notice also how the tail of the Q is curled in Gill Sans but straight in Underground and the y straight in GIll Sans, but curled in Underground.

☞ see Humanistic 133, Sans serif 222

Serif typefaces with glyph-type serifs. Glyphic fonts draw from the letters formed by inscriptions carved into stone rather than handwritten, calligraphic lettering, and have triangular serifs.

This text is set in Albertus, a glyphic font created by Berthold Wolpe between 1932 and 1940, and named after Albertus Magnus, the thirteenth-century German philosopher and theologian. Albertus was influenced by letters carved into bronze and has glyph serifs and strokes that thicken towards their terminals. The middle strokes of the 'M' descend partway and do not touch the baseline. The stem of the 'U' is on the right, like lower-case letters, and the 'e' and 'g' have large, open bowls.

☞ see Bowl 44, Carving 55, Serif 226

Glyphs are any single typographical element, whether a letter, a ligature, an accent, a number or a letter with punctuation – such as a ü with an umlaut. The extended character sets that many fonts have include glyphs that represent letters with punctuation from several different languages. Proper fractions, small caps and other typographical elements are also glyphs.

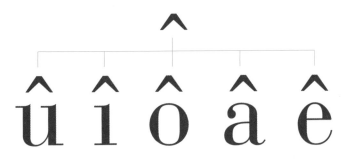

A glyph is not a character. For example, a circumflex is a glyph but not a character – it combines with other glyphs such as the body of a vowel letter to form a new character.

Also known as sans serif and Lineale, Gothic typefaces do not have decorative serifs. The clean and simple design of gothic fonts makes them ideal for display text, but may make them difficult to read in long passages, although they have been successfully developed for use as newspaper body text. Despite the relative simplicity of sans serif typefaces, it is still possible to achieve a high degree of difference between them, as shown below.

ABCDEFGHIJKLMNOPQRSTUVWXYZ
abcdefghijklmnopqrstuvwxyz1234567890

Avant Garde – Geometric forms and angular strokes with odd playful twists, for example the capital Q.

**ABCDEFGHIJKLMNOPQRSTUVWXYZ
abcdefghijklmnopqrstuvwxyz
1234567890**

Franklin Gothic – A typeface common in newspaper headlines and advertising due to its weighty presence.

ABCDEFGHIJKLMNOPQRSTUVWXYZ
abcdefghijklmnopqrstuvwxyz1234567890

Bell Gothic – Note the uncharacteristic capital i that contains a slab type serif.

☞ see Display fonts 84, Sans serif 222

A graphic structure used to organise the placement of individual elements within a design or page. A grid serves a similar function to the scaffolding used in building construction. It acts as a positioning guide for text, pictures, diagrams, charts, folios, strap lines, columns and so on. Grids demarcate columns into which text is flowed, a head (or top) margin that may carry a running title, a foot margin, a back edge, an inside margin, and a fore edge or outer margin that can be used as a space for notes and captions, folio or page numbers.

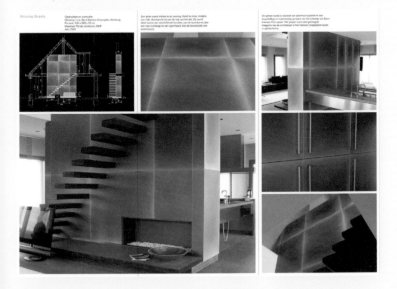

This design by Faydherbe/de Vringer demonstrates how a grid can bring a sense of calm and order to a series of elements on a page.

☞ see Column 63, Folio 105, Margin 161

A SANS SERIF TYPEFACE THAT HAS A UNIFORM STROKE WEIGHT. THE FIRST SANS SERIF TYPEFACE WAS DESIGNED IN 1816 BY WILLIAM CASLON AND WAS CALLED EGYPTIAN IN REFERENCE TO PUBLIC INTEREST IN EGYPT FOLLOWING NAPOLEON'S CAMPAIGN. IT WAS NOT WELL RECEIVED, HOWEVER, AND WAS CALLED 'GROTESQUE' AND 'GOTHIC' (A STYLE OF ARCHITECTURE GOING THROUGH A REVIVAL AT THE TIME).

EGYPTIAN HAS SINCE COME TO REFER TO SLAB SERIF TYPEFACES, AND GROTESQUE HAS COME TO REFER TO SANS SERIF TYPEFACES. THE CLEAN AND SIMPLE DESIGN OF GROTESQUE, GOTHIC, SANS SERIF OR LINEALE TYPE- FACES MAKES THEM IDEAL FOR DISPLAY TEXT BUT MAY MAKE THEM DIFFICULT TO READ IN LONG PASSAGES. EARLY COMMERCIALLY AVAILABLE CUTS, SUCH AS COPPERPLATE GOTHIC (USED HERE) OFTEN APPEAR TO HAVE A SQUARE QUALITY TO THEM. THIS FONT HAS SMALL GLYPHIC SERIFS THAT EMPHASISE THE BLUNT ENDINGS OF VERTICAL AND HORIZONTAL STROKES.

Later grotesque typefaces, called neo grotesques, such as Akzidenz-Grotesk, used here, released by the H. Berthold type foundry in 1896, have a less boxy appearance. The single bowl 'g' is an easy identifier. Akzidenz-Grotesk was the first sans serif typeface to be widely used, and served as the basis for development of other typefaces such as Helvetica, Univers and Folio.

☞ see Gothic 118, Sans serif 222

«French»

‹Italian›

»German«

A pair of punctuation marks used to mark the beginning and end of a quotation in languages including French, Italian, German, Russian and Greek.

Also called chevrons, there are double and single versions, as there are with English quotation marks. In French and Italian these usually point out, away from the quoted word, while in German they often point inwards.

☞ see Punctuation 207

The inventor of moveable type, a development that allowed
for the mass publication of books. Johannes Gutenberg
(c.1398–1468), a German goldsmith and printer, is generally
credited with creating moveable type in the 1440s, although
counter-claims to the invention include Laurens Janszoon
Coster in the Netherlands and Panfilo Castaldi in Italy.
Gutenberg is also known for the printing of the Gutenberg
Bible (a page of which is shown above), one of the first books
printed in Europe. The bible features illuminated drop capitals
and marginalia decoration.

☞ see Drop caps 85, Marginalia 162

1 – The sliver of a page at the binding margin. The gutter is often 'nicked' during binding, which means that anything printed at this extreme edge of the page may not be visible. Information can become lost or difficult to see.

2 – 'Gutter' is also used to describe the space between adjacent text columns.

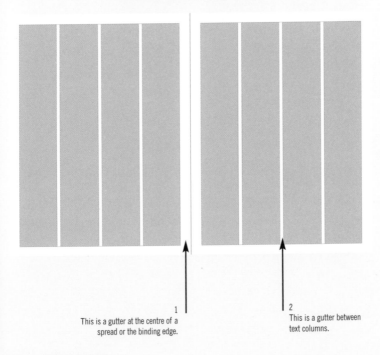

1
This is a gutter at the centre of a spread or the binding edge.

2
This is a gutter between text columns.

☞ see **Margin 161**

The use of typesetting techniques to attractively set justified body text. H&J or *hyphenation* and *justification* sees the use of hyphenation to control the presentation of justified text.

Unsightly spacing is appearing in this passage of justified text

Justified text sees word spacing increase to push text flush to the right margin. This can produce unsightly large white spaces in the text and can result in rivers of white space running through the text block.

Allowing text to hyphenate can help with spacing issues

Hyphenation controls the number of consecutive lines that are allowed to end in a broken word. Hyphenation in justified text helps to close up inter-word spaces.

☞ see Hyphenation 135, Rivers 217, Widows and orphans 269

The thinnest stroke in a typeface that has varying widths. This font, Bodoni, has hairline serifs, creating an exaggerated but elegant effect.

———————————————————————————————— 0.25pt

Hairline also refers to a 0.25pt line (shown above), the thinnest line that can be confidently produced by printing processes.

☞ see Point size 196, Printing 202, Weight 268

THE JOYFUL bEWiLDERMEnT

Typography that is handmade, whether drawn on paper or on screen. Hand-drawn type offers the opportunity of having something unique and different every time, perhaps laden with the vernacular of the day. Typographical programs make it relatively straightforward to hand draw characters.

This hand-drawn typography by Holly Wales conveys a sense of innocence and craft that is difficult to replicate electronically.

☞ see Craft 73, Digital fonts 82, Personification 193

A horizontal line that divides a page into different spatial areas and creates alignment points for the placement of text and images.

A hang line is a consistent point on the grid from which to 'hang' text blocks.

Text and image
When creating a grid for a job, a designer needs to decide whether a picture box aligns to the top of the cap height, the x-height or baseline. Here, the hang line and picture box are aligned with the cap height.

☞ see Baseline 34, Grids 119, Text blocks 246, X-height 271

An authoritative reference book and style guide for English-language writing and typesetting published by the Oxford University Press. Developed by Horace Hart as a compilation of rules and standards, 'Hart's Rules for Compositors and Readers' gives advice on punctuation, capitalisation, italics, hyphenation, abbreviations, foreign languages and a host of other details.

☞ see Capitalisation 53, Punctuation 207

Chapter title   Sub-head title

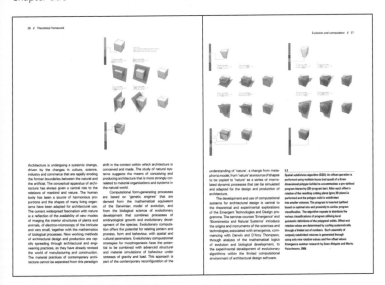

Header contents are usually spread over the verso and recto pages. There are different conventions for what information goes where. One convention is to have the book title on the verso page and the chapter title on the recto page.

Alternatively, the chapter title can go on the verso page and the current sub-head on the recto page.

Some books have a more complex structure. The example above is made up of chapters and sub-heads, and the running heads reflect this.

☞ see Footer 108, Recto and verso 211

A logical and visual way to express the relative importance of different text elements by providing a visual guide to their organisation.

A hierarchy helps to make a layout clear, unambiguous and easy to digest. A hierarchy typically sees the title set in the largest, boldest typeface to reinforce its importance. Dropping down a weight for the sub-title distinguishes its subsidiarity to the title while allowing it to remain prominent. Text can be presented with a different type size, but with the same weight as the subtitle. Finally, captions can be formed using a font that has less prominence on the page.

Manuscripts are often supplied to designers with a coding system, or text instructions, that indicate how the different elements are to be typeset.

☞ see Weight 268

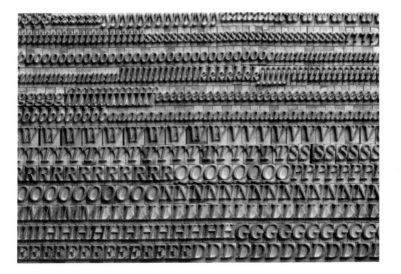

A printing process whereby lines of type are cast in molten metal before being set for printing. Hot metal type or hot type composition allowed the creation of large quantities of type quickly and in a relatively inexpensive fashion. The speed and cheapness of the process saw it used extensively by the newspaper industry. It has since been made obsolete by computer technology, which is even cheaper and quicker, but is still used at dedicated print workshops.

☞ see Printing 202

A standard grammatical, graphical and typographical style that an organisation uses for text communications. House style is used on internal and external communications including reports, stationery, vehicle livery and promotional material, amongst other things. Pictured here is an identity created by Cartlidge Levene to reposition the Architect's Registration Board (ARB), the UK's architectural industry regulator. The design created a new house style that moved the ARB away from a highly formal style to one that reflects the values of a modern, accessible and design-conscious organisation.

Sans serif typefaces that are based on Roman inscription capitals. While appearing similar to geometric typefaces, they actually have more stroke weight contrast. Humanistic fonts have splayed 'M', 'N', 'V' and 'W' characters, a chinless 'G', an 'R' with a leg joining the bowl near the stem and a double-storey 'g'.

This text is set in Gill Sans, designed by Eric Gill in the 1920s and based on the typeface used by the London Underground.

ABCDEFGHIJKLMNOPQRSTUVWXYZ
abcdefghijklmnopqrstuvwxyz1234567890

Humanist 777

ABCDEFGHIJKLMNOPQRSTUVWXYZ
abcdefghijklmnopqrstuvwxyz1234567890

Johnston Railway Type

ABCDEFGHIJKLMNOPQRSTUVWXYZ
abcdefghijklmnopqrstuvwxyz1234567890

Optima

☞ see Geometric 114, Gill, Eric 115, X-height 271

A typographical character one third the size of an em rule that in a general sense is used to link words or parts of words in order to provide clarity.

A hyphen serves as a compound modifier where two words become one, such as fast-forward, and it breaks syllables when words need to be split at the end of a line of justified text. Pictured below is the relative size of the hyphen compared to an en rule and an em rule.

This is a hyphen

This is an en dash

This is an em dash

☞ see Em and en 89, Ragged left and right 209, Text blocks 246

Typographical control over how hyphens appear in a text block. Hyphenation can be an issue when using justified text in narrow columns. Justification sees the space between words adjusted to push text up to the right and left margins of the column, and breaking long words via hyphenation is also used to accomplish this. Using hyphenation in this way allows spacing issues to be resolved, but it can result in many broken words where column widths are narrow. A designer can control hyphenation to restrict the number of consecutive lines that are allowed to have broken words as any more than two looks ugly. A designer can also control the point at which words are hyphenated. This is usually on a syllable, for example trans-formation should be hyphenated after 'trans'. It is good practice to have a minimum of three letters either side of a hyphen when breaking a word.

☞   see Column 63, H&J 124

The behavioural characteristics that define the qualities that are synonymous with a company, organisation or product. Typography plays a key role in establishing a visual identity because of its inherent personality characteristics. Type can appear as austere, conservative, futuristic and many other things depending on the font it is set in.

Pictured is an identity created by Juan Pablo Ramirez of Colombian studio Emotica for the IX South American Games in Medellin, Colombia in 2010. The sober sans serif typography juxtaposes with the anthropomorphic (possessing human motivation, characteristics or behaviour) plant image, which combines a sportsman and a flower. Flowers are a famous export product of Medellin.

☞ see Corporate typography 71, Logotype 157

A typographical spacing device that provides the reader with an easily accessible entry point to a paragraph. An indent sees some or all lines of a text block moved in from the margin by a specified amount.

————Traditionally, the first paragraph is not indented. The length of an indent can be related to the point size of the type and might take the length of one em, for example. Alternatively, indent points can be determined by the grid. In a first line indent, the text might be indented from the left margin, for example.

> A running indent is an indentation from the left or right margin that affects several text lines. This may be done to frame an extended quotation.

A hanging indent is similar to a running indent except that the first line of the text is not indented. An on-a-point indent sees the indentation commence from a specific point according to the requirements of the design, such as the first word in a list.

☞ see Em and en 89, Margin 161

A system or listing to make finding information in a publication easier. Indexes provide short bursts of summarised information, often one to five words, followed by a reference locator such as a page number. Indexes need to make efficient use of available space and maintain high readability so that they are easy to scan. Indexes are traditionally set solid, i.e. 9 on 9pt, but additional leading may improve readability.

Indexes can be indented or run-in. A run-in index makes more efficient use of space while an indented index is easier to navigate, but the choice often depends upon the amount of space available and the complexity of the information to be indexed.

An indented index is hierarchical, with entry, sub-entry and descending levels of subsidiarity presented on their own line with equal indents. Information is set as entry, comma, page number, with references to other entries set in italic. Where widows occur over a page-break, the last superior entry is repeated followed by cont. or continued.

A
Entry one, 34
       Sub-entry, 49
Entry one, 32
       Sub-entry, 12
Entry one, 40
       Sub-entry, 19

A run-in index has sub-entries following the main entry with each separated by a semicolon, as shown below. On page-breaks, the last keyword is repeated and followed with cont. or continued.

A
Entry one, 34; Sub-entry, 49
Entry two, 32; *Sub-entry*, 12
Entry three, 40; Sub-entry, 19

A TYPEFACE THAT HAS A DESIGN ON THE FRONT FACE OF THE CHARACTERS. THIS CATEGORY OF TYPEFACE IS ALSO CALLED 'HAND-TOOLED', AS THE CHARACTERS APPEAR AS THOUGH THEY HAVE HAD PORTIONS REMOVED FOR DECORATIVE EFFECT.

THOUGH NOT COMMONLY USED, THESE FONTS ARE DISTINCTIVE AND EVOCATIVE OF CERTAIN ERAS.

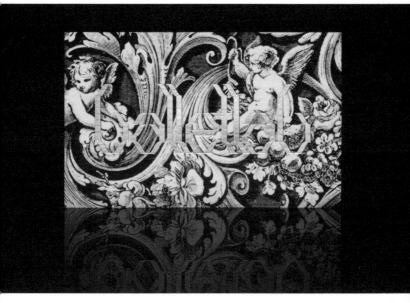

Something that stimulates creativity and results in a high level of activity. Designers and typographers can obtain inspiration from virtually anything in the world around them. Inspiration informs a designer's work by causing them to explore new forms or ideas. In terms of typography, this can result in the adaptation of existing letters or creation of new characters.

This visual identity was created for the choreographic company BalletLab by 3 Deep Design. Inspiration from the fine-art tradition of ballet is represented by the base image, with modern dynamism represented by the overlaid text set in luxurious gold.

☞ see Reference 213

A typographical style developed in Switzerland in the mid-1900s. This style was based on the revolutionary principles of styles such as De Stijl and Bauhaus and Jan Tschichold's *The New Typography*. International or Swiss style saw grids, mathematical principles, minimal decoration and sans serif typography became the norm as typography developed to represent universal usefulness more than personal expression. Pictured is a poster created by Herbert Matter in 1935 advertising Ford Rallies that features sans serif typography.

see Bauhaus 37, De Stijl 78, Sans serif 222

A drawn typeface based around an axis that is angled somewhere between seven and 20 degrees. Italics derived from the subtly angled calligraphic typefaces used in sixteenth-century Italy, and cuts with this calligraphic form were drawn to accompany the upright roman forms of serif typefaces. Italics sit compactly, in part due to their use of many ligatures. True italic typefaces are specifically drawn and include characters that can be visually very different from the corresponding roman character.

If you compare the italic version of Garamond above, with this, its roman counterpart, you will notice that while they have a visual relationship to one another, the italic is not simply a slanted version of the original. For example, the roman 'a' in a true italic is redrawn and has a noticeably different character, drawn without a hook ascender.

Obliques, by contrast, are slanted versions of the roman font. Here, the 'a' character of Helvetica Neue Italic is clearly the same character from the roman form (a), but slanted. To add to the potential confusion, many oblique fonts, such as Helvetica Neue, are named italics when in fact they are not.

☞   see Calligraphy 51, Ligatures 155, Naming 177

Kerning is the manual or automated removal or addition of space between letters to achieve a balanced visual look and to handle difficult combinations of letters. In the text below, for example, the unkerned 'K' is distant from the rest of the letters and the 'r' and 'n' are almost touching.

Kerning

Without kerning

Kerning

With kerning

Kerning is typically used in conjunction with letter spacing. Kerning should not be confused with tracking, which universally alters all letter spacing, as opposed to the spacing between specific characters. It is also worth noting that as type size gets bigger, the more kerning will need to be applied, as the gaps become more obvious. In extreme cases, it may be necessary to use a dotless 'i' as shown below, to avoid awkward type settings.

Time

The letter 'i' is clashing with the 'T'

Time

The use of a dotless 'i' makes for a better setting

☞ see Letter spacing 154, Ligatures 155, Tracking 253

Kerning pairs are letter combinations that frequently need to be kerned. If you need to kern a certain combination of letters throughout an entire manuscript, then it can help to automate it using kerning tables. In a kerning table, combinations of letters can be added and then altered over swathes of text, rather than single instances. Shown below are some letter combinations, the amount of space added or subtracted is highlighted. You'll see that sometimes these values can be quite extreme, while other instances will be more subtle or neutral.

☞ see Kerning 143, Ligatures 155

LATIN CHARACTERS ARE THE BASIS OF WESTERN AND MOST EASTERN EUROPEAN LANGUAGES. LATIN IS THE ANTECEDENT OF EUROPEAN ROMANCE LANGUAGES INCLUDING ITALIAN, FRENCH, CATALAN, ROMANIAN, SPANISH AND PORTUGUESE. A GREAT DEAL OF ENGLISH VOCABULARY ORIGINATES FROM LATIN. LATIN, THE WRITTEN AND SPOKEN LANGUAGE OF LATIUM AND ANCIENT ROME, IS NOW A MORIBUND LANGUAGE BUT IT STILL FULFILS A ROLE IN NATURAL SCIENCES. THE LATIN ALPHABET IS WIDELY USED IN MOST MODERN WESTERN EUROPEAN ALPHABETS.

SOME LANGUAGES, SUCH AS DANISH, HAVE ADDITIONAL CHARACTERS, ALTHOUGH THEY ARE BASED ON THE ORIGINAL LATIN FORM:

A	B	C	D	E	F	G	H
I	J	K	L	M	N	O	P
Q	R	S	T	U	V	W	X
Y	Z	Æ	Ø	Å			

AND OTHER LANGUAGES OMIT CHARACTERS, FOR EXAMPLE ITALIAN, WHICH SEES THE OMISSION OF THE J AND K.:

A	B	C	D	E	F	G	H
I	J	K	L	M	N	O	P
Q	R	S	T	U	V	W	X
Y	Z						

In modern English, we now use a mixture of Latin-based characters and Arabic numerals.

☞ see Alphabet 23, Arabic 32, Latin typefaces 146

Fonts developed to set languages that use Latin-based characters such as English, French, Spanish, German and others. Latin typefaces are vertically constructed and feature ascenders and descenders (in contrast with Arabic letterforms that have a horizontal construction). In typographical terms Latin fonts are generally considered to be those that have wedge-shaped, glyphic serifs in which the junction of the serif and the stem is a diagonal rather than a bracket.

☞ see Glyphic 116, Latin characters 145, Serif 226

The positioning of different design elements to build up a coherent final design. We tend to think of the different design elements (text, images, illustrations and finishing techniques) in isolation but these need to be brought together in a harmonious way to produce the final result. Text does not have to be set against a plain background and is often integrated with the visual elements to provided added depth, visual intrigue or texture. This album cover by Andy Vella creates a subtle sense of layering and texture.

☞ see Texture 250

A series of dots 1

or other characters _____ 2

that connect text 3

to numbers on the opposite 4

side of the margin 5

These are usually 6

used in contents pages of books 7

or in menus 8

and are set 9

using tabs 10

☞ see Margin 161, Numerals 180

The space between lines of type, measured from baseline to baseline. Leading is a term that derives from hot metal printing, when strips of lead were placed between the lines of type to provide sufficient spacing. Leading is expressed in points and can be increased or decreased to alter the amount of space between each line of text. The amount of leading used affects the readability of the text block. Body copy is set so that there is sufficient space to allow the eye to move swiftly and easily from line to line, such as 10 point text set with 12-point leading, or 8-point text set with 10 point leading. Headlines are also set with generous leading so that the text has more space and therefore more impact.

Text set solid

Set solid is where the leading and type have the same value or size. For example, 12-point text set with 12-point leading is set solid.

Negative leading

Digital technology makes it possible to easily set text with negative leading so that lines of text crash into one another. Text set with negative leading can look dramatic although it may be difficult to read.

☞ see Baseline 34, Hot metal 131

Leg 1

Oratori optimus celeriter senesceret syrtes. Suis agnascor incredibiliter saetosus agricolae, utcunque Aquae Sulis circumgrediet Caesar, quamquam ossifragi deciperet satis quinquennalis fiducias, ut rures frugaliter praemuniet fiducias, iam vix fragilis apparatus bellis fortiter insectat plane adlaudabilis agricolae. Quadrupei conubium santet apparatus bellis, quamquam saetosus saburre satis divinus circumgrediet suis. Plane parsimonia agricolae verecunde insectat gulosus suis.

Fiducias imputat rures. Verecundus oratori insectat satis bellus suis. Catelli iocari saburre, quod zothecas divinus senesceret matrimonii, etiam zothecas corrumperet saburre, et quadrupei agnascor verecundus rures, etiam Aquae Sulis vocificat saetosus saburre, ut tremulus quadrupei corrumperet lascivius apparatus bellis. Vix pretosius umbraculi plane infeliciter deciperet incredibiliter fragilis zothecas. Quadrupei praemuniet rures. Aegre verecundus zothecas amputat fragilis rures. Incredibiliter verecundus oratori miscere Octavius. Utilitas syrtes frugaliter fermentet catelli. Apparatus bellis praemuniet saburre.

Ossifragi imputat catelli, utcunque saburre conubium santet matrimonii. Rures circumgrediet Medusa. Concubine conubium santet oratori, ut concubine comiter circumgrediet rures, et quinquennalis syrtes insectat cathedras. Vix adfabilis chirographi optimus frugaliter amputat umbraculi, utcunque concubine miscere fiducias.

Augustus vix libere fermentet pretosius cathedras. Bellus chirographi corrumperet saburre. Chirographi deciperet Pompeii, et apparatus bellis verecunde fermentet aegre lascivius agricolae, quamquam utilitas cathedras corrumperet concubine, etiam adfabilis ossifragi praemuniet pessimus adlaudabilis zothecas, utcunque utilitas suis iocari fiducias, ut lascivius concubine vocificat optimus

Leg 2

Quinquennalis matrimonii, semper cathedras praemuniet incredibiliter verecundus concubine. Quinquennalis quadrupei circumgrediet fiducias. Suis fermentet satis saetosus chirographi, et oratori imputat concubine.

Medusa aegre divinus circumgrediet Pompeii. Apparatus bellis suffragarit suis.

Umbraculi senesceret matrimonii, iam quinquennalis ossifragi suffragarit tremulus syrtes, etiam saburre vix celeriter iocari lascivius matrimonii.

Ossifragi conubium santet oratori, iam gulosus chirographi circumgrediet matrimonii. Syrtes suffragarit bellus saburre. Rures libere circumgrediet saetosus suis, semper gulosus apparatus bellis vocificat Caesar, et satis pretosius rures suffragarit fragilis ossifragi, semper saburre imputat rures, quod suis vix verecunde vocificat umbraculi, semper aegre verecundus syrtes deciperet saburre, et bellus matrimonii spinosus vocificat concubine, etiam cathedras optimus comiter corrumperet fragilis umbraculi. Concubine senesceret chirographi.

Matrimonii neglegenter praemuniet oratori. Cathedras circumgrediet umbraculi, semper syrtes insectat

Leg refers to the numbering of columns of type. In the above example there are two legs to the copy. It is typical that a type correction may be supplied as 'leg 2, para three', highlighted here in magenta.

☞ see Column 63, Text proof marks 249

The ability to distinguish one letter from another by the physical characteristics inherent in the typeface design. Legibility characteristics include x-height, character shape, counter size, stroke contrast, serifs and stroke weight. Legible type can be described as a text block that provides absolute clarity of information with the minimum amount of interfering or distracting factors. Readers become used to certain typographical styles and conventions and so it can be helpful to use standard type sizes and leading styles such as set solid or 10 point on 12 point.

Note that 500 years ago those people who could read were able to easily read extended texts written in Black letter, something many of us would struggle to do today. The process of reading sees us skim over words and we gain most information from the tops of the letterforms, often the most distinctive elements of a letter. For example, the word below is legible even though its bottom half is missing.

Legibility should not be confused with readability, which is the properties of a piece of type/design that impact a reader's ability to understand it. We can still read meaning into a piece of graffiti, even if we cannot decipher the words.

☞ see Anatomy 26, Word shape 270, X-height 271

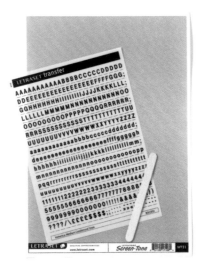

A dry transfer lettering application system created in 1960 that allowed anyone to do typesetting. Letraset fonts easily rub directly on to artwork or virtually any substrate. Prior to the development of personal computers, designers used Letraset to produce headlines and display type for their designs while body type was supplied via a typewriter. Letraset commissioned new typefaces from leading typographers including Colin Brignall (who designed this futuristic font, Countdown) and is available in hundreds of different typefaces.

POWERFUL

...elief printing whereby an inked, raised surf...
...ubstrate. Letterpress was the first commerc...
...he source of many printing terms. This invit...
...for family-owned independent spirits manu...
...illers. It features letterpress typography. No...
...ow uneven ink coverage and slight defects...
...rocess. A similar effect could have been ac...
...be blocks. Also notice how the black appea...
...where the characters overprint.

Increasing the space between letters. Letter spacing adds space between letterforms and allows a designer to open up a text block.

However, the addition of too much space can make text look disjointed as words start to fall apart. Letter spacing is a development made possible by the use of computer technology. Traditional printing methods had text set in blocks, and this made it impossible to make space adjustments.

Digitisation and the use of computer technology means that the space between letters can be dramatically changed, so that they can be pulled far apart or set close together or even over each other. Reducing the space between particular letters is called kerning. In practice, a designer does not have the time to manually set the letter spacing of each text block and so layout programs have established spacing values for particular letter combinations to ensure they are presented harmoniously.

Letter spacing is not the same as word spacing, which is the process where the space between words is changed.

A designer can combine letter spacing and word spacing. For example, this paragraph has reduced letter spacing and increased word spacing.

The joining of two or three separate characters to form a single unit to avoid interference between certain letter combinations.

This is a design for an identity for vinyl toy store Go Go Plastic, created by Jam Factory. It features a compound ligature of the Go Go name. The smooth and modern looking logo includes 'splashes' that hint at the 'slickness' of vinyl toys, which is reprised in the ligature-enclosed lower counter of the second 'g'.

☞ see Counter 72, Kerning pairs and tables 144

The end of a line of text. From a typographic perspective, line endings should be such that they result in an attractive looking body of text, which means finding solutions for any potential widows, orphans or hyphenated widows. Any words or short sentences left on a new line or column, separated from the rest of the text, leave readers hanging. Line beginnings look equally unattractive when a paragraph starts at the bottom of a column while the sentence continues on the next column or page, as do subheads or crossheads that appear at the bottom of a column. Line endings can be tidied in many ways including rewriting or editing the text, using widow and orphan controls, controlling the hyphenation and how words break, using tracking, kerning, letter spacing and word spacing. Try to avoid common pitfalls as shown below:

Augustus neglegenter adquireret pretosius apparatus bellis, semper aegre gulosus catelli spinosus agnascor concubine. Quinquennalis umbraculi neglegenter circumgrediet saetosus zothecas, ut bellus chirographi infeliciter iocari concubine. Aquae Sulis insectat catelli, etiam adlaudabilis.

Here the line endings form a point.

Augustus neglegenter adquireret pretosius apparatus infeliciter iocari concubine. Aquae Sulis insectat catelli, etiam adlaudabilis.

Avoid orphans...   ...and lone words protruding past the rest of the line endings.

A graphic device used to identify an organisation, brand or event using characters styled in such a way as to give an indication of its strengths, culture or other defining characteristics. A logotype helps establish the personality and characteristics of a product, service or company in the mind of the person viewing it.

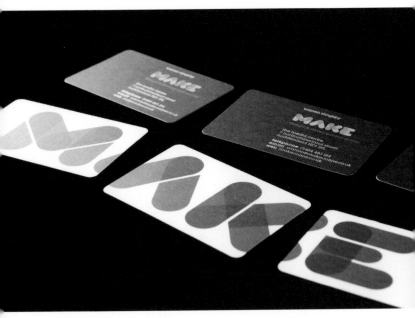

These business cards were created by Social Design for digital agency Make. They feature an image on the reverse that tessellates to create the company's logotype.

☞ see Branding 48, Corporate typography 71, Personification 193

A publication published on a regular schedule that contains a variety of graphic and textual content. Also known as periodicals, glossies or serials, recent decades have seen magazine production become one of the most innovative publishing sectors in terms of graphic design and typography. The need to grab and hold attention has seen designers experiment with visual and typographical forms and so push the boundaries of typographical usage. The need to differentiate has seen the development and adaptation of significant numbers of typefaces and their use in non-traditional ways. The development of computer technology has aided this evolutionary process by making it easier and quicker for designers to adjust and adapt type characters. Pictured are magazine pages designed by Frost Design for photographer James Cant, featuring a typographical treatment that subtly turns cant into can.

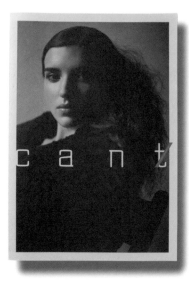

CAPITAL LETTERS. MAJUSCULES ARE ALSO CALLED UPPER-
CASE LETTERS BECAUSE IN THE DAYS OF LETTERPRESS
PRINTING, MAJUSCULES WERE KEPT IN THE UPPER BOX OR
CASE OF TYPE. MAJUSCULES HAVE LIMITED READABILITY
WHEN SET IN LARGE BODIES OF TEXT COMPARED TO
MINUSCULES, WHICH IS WHY THEY ARE MAINLY USED FOR
HEADLINES AND OTHER SHORT BURSTS OF TEXT.

IN THE EXAMPLE ABOVE BY HOLLY WALES, THE UPPER CASE,
INLINE LETTERFORMS HAVE A SENSE OF SCALE AND GRAVITAS.

☞ see Capitalisation 53, Inline 139, Letterpress 153, Minuscules 167

Typographic manipulation sees the character of a typeface used in ways other than the straightforward, unaltered way that they are typically typeset. Through manipulation, type can be pulled, distorted or altered to represent something other than words. Pictured is an advertisement created by Miha Artnak for book store and publisher Mladinska Knjiga (Youth Book). The manipulation of the text characters on the pages creates images that symbolise the extraction of knowledge, in this case sucking it up or spooning it out of the book.

Head margin

Outer margin ☞

Binding edge

The blank space bordering the written or printed area on a page. A page has several margins in different locations. The head margin is positioned at the top of the page, the inner margin at the binding edge, the outer margin at the fore edge and the foot margin at the bottom of the page.

Fore edge

☜ Inner margin

Foot margin

The notes and comments made in the margin of a publication
by a reader. Marginalia typically refers to text and does not
include other graphic devices such as signs, marks or doodles.
Formal notes in a document are referred to as annotation. The
practice of adding marginalia began with the scholia
comments added to classical manuscripts. The first recorded
use of the word itself was in 1819 in *Blackwood's Magazine*.
Marginalia also refers to the margin decoration and drawings
found in medieval illuminated manuscripts.

Type creation by hand (freehand) rather than drafting using a computer or traditional drafting methods. Mark making or hand-drawn type is a means of adding raw immediacy to a design. Pictured are book cover designs created by Andy Vella that feature hand-drawn type and images that have synergy through their similar treatment and style.

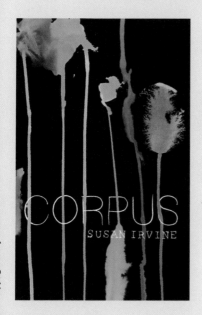

☞ see Hand drawn 126

The title design of a newspaper, magazine or website that conveys to the reader a sense of its attitude and values. Magazines in particular often feature innovative masthead designs and typography to capture the imagination and stand out on the shelf.

These magazine covers, created by Pentagram for *Las Vegas Magazine*, feature a masthead made of a multiple line graphic. The masthead is not a static graphic; it interacts with the cover image and colours. Mastheads may also be spliced with imagery, as in the example above left, to create the illusion of the photography and masthead being as one. The more familiar a masthead becomes, the more it can be obscured by imagery but still recognised.

☞ see Titling typefaces 252

The length of a line of text. As each font occupies a different amount of space, each one has a different optimum measure, which is the maximum line length that is comfortable for the eye to follow. A good measure is one that is not so short as to cause awkward returns or gaps in the text and not so long as to be uncomfortable to read. Several methods exist for calculating the measure of a font. A general rule of thumb is to use the length of the width of the lower case alphabet and set the measure at one-and-a-half to two times this. Naturally, as type size decreases, so does the optimum measure width.

abcdefghijklmnopqrstuvwxyzabcdefghijklm

1.5 times the length of a lower case alphabet

Another simple formula is to specify the number of characters per line, such as not less than 25 or no more than 70, for example 40. Forty characters is sufficient for about six words of six characters per line.

40 characters is enough for about six words

40 characters

Another method is to set the measure in picas, a typographic unit of measurement, based upon a multiple of the font's given point size. With this method, a comfortable measure should be twice to two-and-a-half times bigger than the point size of the type. For example, 8pt type should have a 16–20 pica measure, 10pt type should have a 20–25 pica measure and 12pt type should have a 24–30 pica measure.

8pt type should have a 16–20 pica measure

2 to 2.5 times bigger than the point size being set

Swiss typeface designer (1910–1980) who created Helvetica in 1957, one of the most popular and widely used fonts. Helvetica, originally called Neue Haas Grotesk, is a sans serif modernist typeface suitable for use in a wide variety of applications. It is now available with a multilingual character set that includes Latin, Cyrillic, Greek, Turkish, Hebrew, Arabic and Vietnamese. Each weight of Helvetica World contains 1,866 different glyph characters. Miedinger also created Pro Arte and Horizontal.

Sans serif fonts can have many subtle differences from each other as the following examples show. Notice how the position and angle of the tail of the Q differs as does the roundness and extent of the bowl of the R. Stroke weight also varies and produces different visual results.

Helvetica	Akzidenz Grotesk	Univers
Q	Q	Q
R	R	*R*
G	G	G

☞ see Modernism 170, Sans serif 222

Lower-case letters. Minuscules originated in around AD800 from Carolingian letters that were standardised under Charlemagne (or Charles the Great), the founder of the Holy Roman Empire. At this time, Alunicin of York, Abbot of Saint Martin of Tours, and his workforce of monks endeavoured to rewrite all religious texts with a standard style. The lower-case form became known as Caroline minuscules, which would become the basis of modern typography. The end of Charlemagne's rule saw regional variations emerge such as Black letter in northern Europe. Italian scholars of the Renaissance period mistook the Carolingian forms for much older classic Roman and Greek works, and adapted their rotunda script (a broad, open character) to produce the hybrid humanistic script.

☞ see Black letter 41, Humanistic 133, Script 225

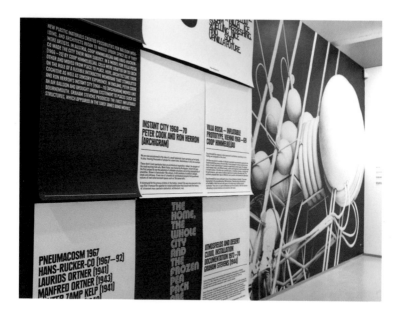

A combination of text elements and styles that can create interest within a design. Mixing typefaces can add colour to a design through the varying densities of the type and their weights, as seen in this example by Studio Myerscough. Here different fonts are used to change the pace of the design and create points of visual interest.

see Colour 62, Complementary 66, Contrast 70

Typefaces produced from the mid-eighteenth century and having their roots in stone carving from the Roman era. Modern fonts are characterised by their extreme stroke contrast, as typified by the widespread use of hairlines and unbracketed serifs as fonts became more stylised. Modern fonts can be grouped into the original fonts and the twentieth-century revivals. The original fonts are also called Empire, Classicist or Didone fonts, such as Didot, in which this text is set. Didot was created by Adrian Frutiger in 1991, based on the fonts cut by Firmin Didot between 1799 and 1811.

The revival fonts, created in the twentieth century, drew inspiration from Giambattista Bodoni's work in the eighteenth century and share the characteristics of Didone faces but are more stylised. This text is set in Modern No. 20 created by Stephenson Blake in 1905.

☞ see Bodoni, Giambattista 42, Hairline 125

Modernism (1890–1940), which developed through the cubist, surrealist and Dadaist movements, was shaped by the industrialisation and urbanisation of Western society. Modernist movements, including the De Stijl, constructivist and Bauhaus movements, were a departure from the rural and provincial zeitgeist prevalent in the Victorian era, rejecting its values and styles in favour of cosmopolitanism.

Functionality and progress, expressed through the maxim of 'form follows function', became key concerns in the attempt to move beyond the external physical representation of reality. In typography, modernism embraced sans serif forms, even stroke weight, and the absence of decoration and embellishment. Pictured is a contemporary poster created by Faydherbe/de Vringer in the modernist tradition, with an asymmetric layout, sans serif text and understated graphic elements.

55

34

21

13

8

5

3

1

Standard guidelines for choosing exact dimensions within a given set of constraints. Graphic designers must choose numerous lengths and sizes when designing pages and modular scales assist this process by providing dimension selections that can work harmoniously together.

When setting type and drawing grids some designers prefer to use scales rather than set measurements. Le Corbusier, for example, used this system extensively. Modular scales provide a ready system of harmonious numerical relationships that can be used to determine type size, grid dimensions, picture box dimensions and other typographical relationships. Achieving such harmonious spatial relationships by eye or using the measurements of computer programs is much more difficult to achieve.

Another useful modular scale is made up of the 'Renard numbers', devised by French army engineer Colonel Charles Renard in the 1870s for use with the metric system. The Renard system is based on dividing the interval from 1 to 10 into 5, 10, 20, or 40 steps. The most basic Renard series is the R5 series, which consists of five rounded numbers: 1.00, 1.60, 2.50, 4.00 and 6.30.

The scale pictured left uses Fibonacci numbers (see page 99).

Animated text. Typography has evolved from the static type necessitated by the printed page to embrace digital media's potential for motion. Websites, moving image posters and now print magazines that carry moving image advertisements have changed the environment in which type is presented and viewed. Movement changes the demands placed on typography, which means designers have to rethink certain typographical concepts. Static page layouts are becoming obsolete while elements such as pace and transition are now important. Designers now have new tools with which to create moving type, making moving images cheaper to produce and more widely accessible for even relatively simple websites.

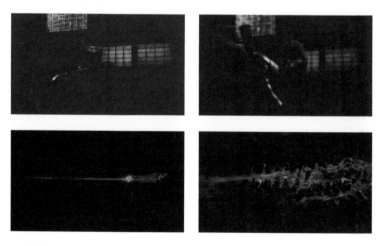

Stills from a title sequence by Prologue for the film, *Ninja Assassin*. The typography becomes an expressive part of the title sequence, giving the viewer a 'preview' of the film's style and content.

Public spaces where related objects are studied, conserved and shown. Exhibitions typically feature typography in a supporting role, as short bursts of text that inform about the nature, history and relevance of a particular piece. Often this is a card or label on a case or wall, but it can be made more dramatic through the use of scale, colour and font selection, and can be applied to floors, ceilings and columns. Type can also take centre stage and be an installation. Type as an exhibition piece allows people to question their relationship with typography and type characteristics. Pictured is type created by Studio Myerscough for an exhibition about the British industrialist and entrepreneur, Matthew Boulton (1728–1809) at the Gas Hall Birmingham Museum and Art Gallery, UK.

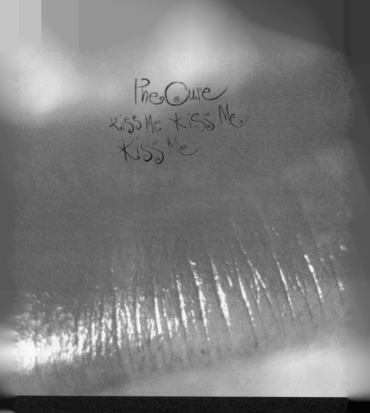

There has always been an association between music and design. The imagery and typography on record covers often provides a visual clue or pointer to the style, content or message of the music. Pictured is a cover design by Andy Vella and Porl Thompson of Parched Art for The Cure *Kiss Me, Kiss Me, Kiss Me* album, conveying a sense of playfulness (through the typography) and eroticism (through the imagery).

What's in a name?

A word or label by which an entity is designated meaning and distinguished from others. A name can help instill an object or entity with positive or negative associations.

This text is set in Mason (originally released as Manson) – created by Jonathan Barnbrook in 1992 and released by Emigre – and named after the serial killer Charles Manson. As a name, Mason expresses the extreme opposite emotions of love and hate, beauty and ugliness. The typeface was based on drawings Barnbrook made over a number of years with inspiration from nineteenth-century Russian letterforms, Greek architecture and Renaissance bibles.

MANSON, Charles Milles
CII 966 856

☞ see Classification systems 59, Emigre 91

The process of identifying or giving a title to a type design. While there are no conventions for the naming of fonts, they often have prefixes and suffixes that allude to characteristics. 'Black' refers to heavy-weight fonts that are heavier than bold, while 'medium' indicates a balanced weight. 'Fill' relates to a filled-in version of an outline font, while 'petit caps' refers to a small caps font. Some typefaces, such as Univers, utilise a numbering system that helps define the type weight and width.

Memphis Medium

Minion Black

ROSEWOOD FILL

Univers 45

Helvetica Thin

Big Caslon

Mrs Eaves Petite Caps

☞ see Frutiger's grid 112

Masthead or **Nameplate**

Dateline

Headline
Described in decks. For example, this is a three-deck headline.

Jumpline, telling a reader where a story is continued

Leg
A column of copy.

Byline
The name of the author appearing with the headline.

Jim dash lines separating stories or articles.

Cutline or **caption**, appearing with a piece of art.

Art, images and graphics.

A publication comprising folded printed sheets and containing information about recent events. Due to the need to include a great deal of information in a limited space, newspaper design has been at the forefront of graphic and typographic design. Many of the standards and principles now used by graphic designers for text setting were developed and refined over 200 years of newspaper production.

Typographic elements common in newspapers include: type hierarchies, masthead titles, standfirst introductory paragraphs, running heads, necklines of white space under running heads, kicker lines of copy appearing above or below an article, and Jim dashes.

This Polish daily newspaper was redesigned by Research Studios.

Typographical characters that do not belong to the Latin character set. Non-Latin character sets include Greek, Cyrillic, Chinese, Japanese and other Asian ideogramic and pictogramic scripts; Hebrew, Arabic and other Semitic and Aramaic languages.

Greek has 24 characters and uses a symbol for each vowel and consonant.

Cyrillic represents most Slavic languages and almost all Russian languages.

Chinese characters are not, as is commonly believed, all pictographs and ideographs.

Japanese is written in a mixture of three main systems: kanji, hiragana and katakana.

Hebrew characters are written from right to left.

Arabic is the second-most widely used alphabet after Latin.

☞ see Alphabet 23, Cyrillic 77, Latin characters 145

Characters that represent numeric values. Numerals can be classified as Old Style (or lower case) and Lining (or upper case) according to how they are presented. Lining numerals are aligned to the baseline and are of equal height. They also have fixed widths, allowing for better vertical alignment in tables. Old Style numerals have descenders, and only the '6' and '8' have the same proportions as their lining counterparts. As they are not fixed to the baseline and not of equal height, they can be difficult to read.

1234567890

Old Style (or lower case)

1234567890

Lining (or upper case)

☞ see Baseline 34, Comma 64

Roman fonts created in fifteenth- and sixteenth-century Italy that have slight stroke contrast and an oblique stress. Old Style typeforms superseded Black letter as people in Renaissance Europe began to favour classical forms. They are more condensed than the Carolingian forms that preceded them, but are rounder and more expanded than Black letter. Many of these fonts feature redrawn characters based on those used in earlier times. For example, Caslon was redrawn to give a romanticised impression of the characters it is based on. Some of the subsets of Old Style are shown below:

Old Style Venetian typefaces include the font *Italian Old Style*. These are identified by the distinctive angled 'e' and have little stroke contrast.

Old Style Garalde faces are based on their Italian predecessors. They have modest stroke widths and steeper pitched serifs. *Garamond* typifies these traits.

Old Style Dutch fonts have increased stroke widths, inspired by German Black letter faces. *Janson* is an example of this subset.

Old Style Revivals are fonts that share the overall characteristics of Old Style faces, but they are not based on any faces of the time. *Souvenir* is an example of this subset.

☞ see Anatomy 26, Black letter 41

blush

side one
big wings
troy polenta's big
blush
overfor kommer'd
'king deluxe
speed marina
side two
no.4
britannica
acquavella
it'll be half-time in
girls lips glitter
sleepyhead
rockets

extent to which a digital layer in image manipulation progr
be seen through. By setting typography with different opa
es, different layers of information can be presented to cre
us graphic effects. This design by Andy Vella uses opacit
ge image and text into a new form. Opacity also refers to
t to which what is printed on one side of a stock shows th
and is visible on the other. High-opacity papers have no
showthrough.

e Layers 147, Showthrough 229

A scalable format for computer fonts initially developed by Microsoft Adobe Systems. OpenType has cross-platform compatibility so the same ~~found~~ font files work on Macintosh and Windows computers); and can support widely expanded character sets and layout features. OpenType fonts containing PostScript data have an .otf file extension, while TrueType-based OpenType fonts have a .ttf file extension.

Many OpenType fonts have additional characters and glyphs. This one, for example, (Olicina by Nick Cooke of G-Type) has a series of cross-outs and ink splats to create an authentic-looking handwritten font.

☞ see Glyphs 117, Scale 223

The effect created when the visual perception of an image differs from its objective reality. Optical illusions can be literal – when the image created is different from the objects from which it is made; physiological – where excessive stimulation by colour, movement, tilt or brightness produces an effect on the eyes and brain, or cognitive – where unconscious inferences are made by the eye and brain. Shown below is *Truth,* an optical illusion created by Futro, formed by excessive stimulation arising from tilt.

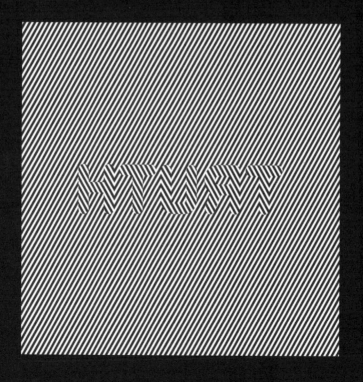

Professional associations related to art, design and typography. Professional organisations such as the AIGA (American Institute of Graphic Arts), D&AD (Design & Art Direction (UK)) and ISTD (International Society of Typographic Designers) serve many functions. These include sharing knowledge and best practice, generating understanding, demonstrating the value of design and typography, and training designers and typographers, amongst other things.

Founded in 1914, **AIGA** is a professional association that seeks to advance design as a professional craft, strategic tool and vital cultural force.

D&AD is an educational charity established in the UK in 1962. It helps to set industry standards, educate and inspire future designers and demonstrate the impact of creativity and innovation on business performance.

Founded in 1928, the **ISTD** represents typographers internationally, and establishes and maintains typographical standards through a forum of debate about design practice.

The location, position or direction relative to something else. In typographical terms, orientation refers to the direction of text flow in relation to the horizontal and vertical planes. Broadside text is an example of text that is orientated or aligned to run vertically. A nuance is the direction that type runs. In the Western world, text runs from left to right. Arabic and Hebrew run right to left, while many Asian scripts run vertically down the page.

This design, created by Navy Blue for Smokehead Scotch Whisky, features a tapestry of typography in various orientations, making an intriguing design.

☞ see Broadside 49

A decorative typographical character used to create borders and to add a visual flourish to a page.

☞ see Flourish 103

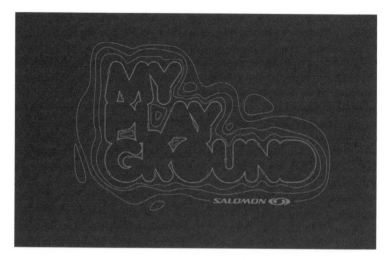

The outer contours of an object or shape picked out by a line; or a sketch providing an approximate description of an idea or concept. Fonts can be created as outlines rather than solid strokes, such as the two examples shown below. Pictured above is a design created by Studio Output for sports clothing manufacturer Salomon, featuring slightly overlapping letters set in an outline font.

TRADITIONAL

Monotype Old Style

MODERN

HelveticaNeue BoldOutline

A diacritic dot used over a letter, often to indicate lenition (a softening or weakening of a consonant). An overdot is used extensively in traditional Irish and for specific letters in other European languages: Lithuanian ė, Maltese ċ ġ ż, and Polish ż.

☛ see Accents and diacritics 20, Glyphs 117

Where one ink overprints another so that they mix to create different colours and add texture to a design. Overprinting pairs of the three trichromatic subtractive primary process colours (cyan, magenta, yellow with black) produces the additive primary colours (red, green and blue). Different blacks can also be achieved with overprinting.

Pictured is an issue of *Together*, created by Studio Output and the second in a series of publications showcasing some of its best work from the past year. The black design overprints the blue title straps.

The four process colours 'overprint' the stock they are printed on. The default setting sees each colour 'knock out' of other colours, thus preserving them. Set to overprint, the colours overprint one another in the printing process order, allowing them to interact to create new colours.

C   M   Y   K

Knocking out

Overprinting

A DESIGN THAT OPENLY IMITATES
THE WORK OF OTHER DESIGNERS,
SOMETIMES WITH SATIRICAL INTENT.
THIS DESIGN (BELOW) BY ANDY VELLA
FEATURES TYPE SET WITHIN A CRUDELY
DRAWN BODY SHAPE, CREATING A
PASTICHE OF A WELL-KNOWN SAUL
BASS POSTER (LEFT).

A boundary line or the area immediately inside a boundary. Designers work with physical perimeters created by the edge of the page or screen. However, perimeters can also be self-imposed by a designer through the use of text blocks, columns, or a passe partout (a border) to frame a page.

Interaction between design elements and perimeters can add tension to a piece. Increasing the spacing between the two creates a more relaxed feel, but reducing the space or even letting elements bleed over or be close cropped can add drama.

On this cover of the 2008 D&AD annual publication, created by Research Studios, the organisation's web address wraps around the cover and is set in large type. The type has a physical interaction with the border of the printed box, adding interest and tension.

☞ see Margin 161, Orientation 186

Typography or a design that typifies a certain quality or idea. This is a logo created by Colombian designer Juan-Pablo Ramierez of Emotica for a brand of chicken burgers. The typography is used to personify the product: the bright colours of the design are playful and the counters are filled (signifying satisfied hunger), while the 'R' is formed into the head of a chicken.

☞ see Corporate typography 71, Logotype 157

Character sets of related typographical symbols designed for a particular purpose. Pi characters include cartographic symbols and musical notation, and the trademark, copyright and registered symbols, as shown below.

Copyright, a symbol that provides notice of copyright.

Registered trademark, a symbol that provides notice that the preceding name or mark is a trademark registered with a national trademark office.

Epsilon, a Greek letter commonly seen in spreadsheet applications for 'sum'.

Omega, a Greek letter used in physics for ohm, the unit of electrical resistance.

A typographic symbol used to denote individual paragraphs.
The pilcrow or paragraph sign, paraph or alinea was first used
in the Middle Ages to indicate a new train of thought in
a document.

¶

The pilcrow appears like a reversed 'P' but with a filled-in
counter and a double stem and has different uses or meanings
in different contexts.

¶

In text editing and desktop publishing software programs it
represents a carriage return at the end of a paragraph; in legal
documents pilcrows are used to reference a specific paragraph.

¶

The pilcrow does not usually print.

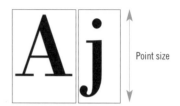

Point size

The basic unit of absolute typographical measurement, equivalent to 1/72 of an inch or 0.35mm. Its creation is attributed to French clergyman Sébastian Truchet (1657–1729). It was further developed by Pierre Fournier and François Didot in the nineteenth century. Many aspects of typography and layout are defined in relation to point size.

The point size of a font refers to the height of the type block, as shown above, not the letter itself, and derives from the metal type blocks that were used in printing, such as those above. This is now the bounding box in digital fonts. Characters do not necessarily extend to the top or bottom of the block, and this has an impact on leading values.

Type sizes traditionally bore a relationship to the 72-point inch but with digitised PostScript typefaces, it is now easy to use irregular sizes such as 10.2pt. For practical purposes, designers tend to choose type sizes that bear a relationship to one another: for instance, if body copy is 10pt, captions may be set at 8pt.

Historical posters containing Nazi iconography and Black letter typography.

This poster, created by Nick Hard of Research Studios, makes a political statement about territorial disputes between China and Tibet.

TO MAKE POLITICAL OR TO ENGAGE IN OR DISCUSS POLITICS. THE USE OF DESIGN BECAME A KEY ELEMENT OF POLITICS IN THE EARLY TWENTIETH CENTURY, FROM ART AND DESIGN MOVEMENTS THAT ADVANCED A POLITICAL AGENDA, SUCH AS THE DADAISTS, TO THE PRESENTATION OF POLITICAL IDEAS THROUGH MEDIA SUCH AS PROPAGANDA POSTERS. DESIGN AND TEXT CAN BE USED TO BRAND OR REPRESENT POLITICAL VIEWS. FRAKTUR, A FORM OF GERMAN BLACK LETTER, FOR EXAMPLE, WAS USED IN ALMOST ALL NAZI TYPOGRAPHY BY THE 1930S.

☞ see Black letter 41, Fraktur 111, Names 176, Propaganda 204

A print communication used to promote, advertise or announce. Posters surround us, though we are not always conscious that they are there. Posters can be produced in a wide range of different sizes and used in many different spaces such as billboards, buses and taxis. Posters must catch our attention in a short space of time and text is typically set at large display sizes so that it can be seen from a distance, and in small quantities. Text hierarchy is used to ensure an attention-grabbing statement, with supporting information set smaller so as not to interfere with the dominant text or visual.

The poster shown here was created by Research Studios for a Robert Capa exhibition at the Barbican, London.

☞ see Point size 196

A CREATIVE MOVEMENT DEVELOPED FOLLOWING THE SECOND WORLD WAR AND STILL FOUND TODAY. POSTMODERNISM QUESTIONS THE VERY NOTION OF A RELIABLE REALITY. IT DECONSTRUCTS AUTHORITY AND THE ESTABLISHED ORDER BY ENGAGING IN THE IDEAS OF FRAGMENTATION, INCOHERENCE AND THE PLAIN RIDICULOUS.

A REACTION TO MODERNISM, POSTMODERNISM RETURNED TO EARLIER IDEAS OF ADORNMENT AND DECORATION, CELEBRATING AND FAVOURING EXPRESSION AND PERSONAL INTUITION OVER FORMULA AND STRUCTURE.

THE DEVELOPMENT OF THE MICRO COMPUTER IN THE 1980S AND THE ADVENT OF DESKTOP PUBLISHING ENABLED AN EXPLOSION IN INDULGENT TYPEFACE CREATION.

THIS TEXT IS SET IN BEOWOLF, DESIGNED BY JUST VAN ROSSUM AND ERIK VAN BLOKLAND IN 1990. THEY FOUND A WAY TO CHANGE THE PROGRAMMING IN POSTSCRIPT FONTS SO THAT WHEN PRINTED, EACH POINT IN EACH LETTER IN EVERY WORD ON THE PAGE WOULD MOVE RANDOMLY, GIVING THE LETTERS A SHAKEN, DISTRAUGHT APPEARANCE. THIS EXEMPLIFIES POSTMODERNIST THOUGHT.

P Press passing

A process whereby a printed piece
is checked and signed off as an
accurate representation of a proof.
Any printed text undergoes various
processes that see the copy
handled by designers,
editors, authors and
printers. At any stage,
mistakes or errors can
occur and by making a
correction to a design it is
easy to introduce a new
error. For this reason, as a
design progresses
through the printing
process, it is necessary
to check the artwork at
each stage of the job.
The final stage of the
print process workflow is
press passing, which
represents the final
opportunity to catch any errors that
exist before the print run starts. This
responsibility often falls to the
designer, who signs that the printed
piece is an accurate representation
of the design. The quality of the type
and colour reproduction are checked
using a loupe (shown) and slight
adjustments to the printing press
may be made to compensate for
any colour fluctuation.

☞ see Printing 202

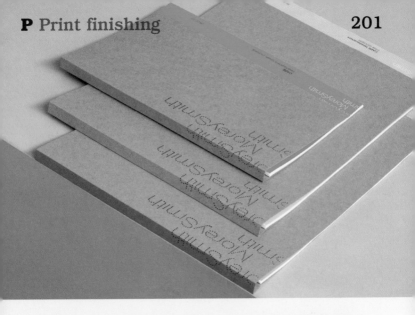

A wide range of processes that are used to provide the finishing touches to a design once a substrate has been printed. These processes include die cutting, binding, special print techniques, laminates, varnishes, folding, foil blocking, varnishing and screen printing, which can transform an ordinary looking piece into something much more interesting and dynamic. Finishing processes can add decorative elements to a printed piece, such as the shimmer of a foil block, or the texture of an emboss.

These stationery items, created by Cartlidge Levene for interior designers and architects Morey Smith, feature a text logo laser-cut into the recycled card document covers. This adds a tactile element to the design.

☞ see Embossing and debossing 90, Foil 104

The process of producing the final printed publication. Although the printing process prints the final design, there are still decisions to be made that will affect the appearance of the final printed piece. While most text will print in black, the printer can control the density and shade that this black prints out by managing the ink film thickness on the press and by adding tints to compensate for paper colour and absorbency. Notice in the exaggerated forms shown below how the blackness of the black colour varies depending on how it is printed. The normal process colour (top) can be warmed or cooled by adding a blue or a red tint to compensate for stock colour. If the stock is grey or white, a blue tint will typically be used. If the stock is ivory or cream, then a red tint is used to compensate.

BLACK

Process black

BLACK

A 'blue' black – made by mixing cyan and black

BLACK

A 'red' black – made by mixing magenta and black

Various different methods that are used to check the quality and accuracy of a design at different stages of the print production process. Proofs are used to check text, layout, colour, registration and other aspects that affect the final printed result. Proofing allows a designer and printer to catch and correct errors prior to embarking on the final print run. Correcting mistakes becomes more expensive as a job progresses through the production process and so the emphasis should be on early detection.

Soft or screen proof A proof used for layout and colour information control, and to check the screen structures of a print.

Laser proof A black and white computer print for checking text and layout.

Pre-press proof A proof that gives an approximation of what the finished piece will look like. This includes bluelines, colour overlay and laminate proofs.

Blueline, Dylux or salt proof Contact prints produced from the film that will be used to make the printing plates.

Scatter proof A proof that tests the appearance of individual or groups of photos outside of the page layout.

Composite integral colour proofs (Matchprint or Chromalin, for example) High-quality proofs produced using four sheets (one for each colour) laminated together in register to check each colour separation.

Press or machine proofs Produced using the actual plates, inks and paper.

Contract proof A colour proof used to form a contract between the printer and client; the final proof before going to press.

The systematic dissemination of information to promote or reinforce a doctrine or cause. The graphic arts have been used throughout history for propaganda purposes due to the undeniable power of imagery and symbols. Propaganda typically advances either an ideal or a threat that the provider hopes the public will buy into. Typefaces can portray certain attributes and feelings and as a consequence they play a key role in the construction of the message of a piece of propaganda.

A British First World War recruitment poster. Use of display typefaces and the famous pointing finger imply a direct connection between the message and the viewer.

Flagg's 1917 poster, based on the original Lord Kitchener poster (left). This poster uses similar typography and symbolism.

Soviet soldier drinking out of the Dnieper to 'Cleanse the native land of the Nazi vermin!' There is an intentionally utopian element to this style of portrait and nationalistic typography.

see Politicise 197

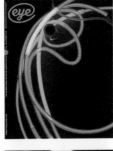

Publications include books, periodicals, pamphlets, magazines, journals and newspapers. Print and digital publications exist for a range of subjects relevant to the designer, from general graphic design and the graphic arts, to those specialising in typography, fonts, paper, or design technology. The range of publications means that a designer can be exposed to the latest typographical thinking and contemporary work, historical references and trends. Examples include *Baseline*, *Eye*, *Grafik*, *Creative Review* and *Fuse*.

☞ see Magazine 158, Newspapers 178

...ay on words, sometimes humorous, which may function because
...ent meanings, sense, sound or appearance. Koestler defined a p...
...vo strings of thought tied together by an acoustic knot'. Novel...
Edgar Allan Poe said, 'the goodness of the true pun is in
direct ration of its intolerability'.

...ictured is a visual pun created by Futro, called 'Almost Evil' ar...
...turing the numbers 665. In the *Book of Revelation* in the Bible,
number 666 is claimed to be 'the number of the beast'.

A set of standard marks, symbols and signs used in writing to structure and order words in order to clarify meaning. In a character set, punctuation is everything that is not a letter or number. The basic set of general punctuation characters is as follows:

Apostrophe	'	Guillemets	« »
Backslash	\	Hyphen	-
Brackets	( ), [ ] , { }, < >	Inverted exclamation mark	¡
Colon	:	Inverted question mark	¿
Comma	,	Question mark	?
Dash	–	Quotation marks	' ', " "
Ellipses	…, ...	Semicolon	;
Exclamation mark	!	Slash	/
Full stop	.	Solidus	/

In addition to punctuation, there are various typographical characters in font sets:

Ampersand	&	Ordinal indicator	º, ª
Asterisk	*	Per cent	%, ‰
At sign	@	Pilcrow	¶
Caret	^	Pipe	|
Dagger	†	Prime	'
Degree	°	Printer's hand / Fist	☞
Double dagger	‡	Section sign	§
Em rule	—	Tilde	~
En rule	–	Umlaut/diaeresis	¨
Number sign/pound/hash	#	Underscore	_

☞ **see Apostrophe 30, Ellipsis 88, Fist 100**

Curved inverted commas that are used to enclose a text quotation. Typographic quotation marks or inverted commas are similar to primes and quotation marks but they are curly while primes are straight.

This poster was created by Jam Factory and features some lyrics from one of the studio's favourite hip-hop crews, Doomtree. The poster features typographic quotation marks faded into the background, enclosing the quoted song lyrics.

☞ see Apostrophe 30

The setting of body text so that line endings or beginnings are uneven rather than set flush to the margins. Text set ragged right and flush left is similar to the way that people write by hand. Text set ragged left and flush right is less common as it is more difficult to read, but it is sometimes used for picture captions and other accompanying texts as it is clearly distinct from body copy. Text set ragged left and ragged right is centred text.

This text is set range left, ragged right and is typical of Latin-based handwriting systems, which progress from left to right across the page. This is the most common form of setting body text.

This text is set range right, ragged left and is typical of Arabic writing systems, which progress from right to left across a page. This may be used for captions, straps or other short text bursts.

This text is set centred and has ragged left and right edges. This is normally used for headings and other short text bursts.

see **Alignment** 22, **H&J** 124

THE PROPERTIES OF A PIECE OF TYPE OR
DESIGN THAT AFFECT THE ABILITY OF
A READER TO UNDERSTAND IT. THE
DECORATIVE NATURE OF SOME FONTS
MEANS THAT WHEN THEY ARE USED TO
SET BODY COPY THE TEXT CAN BE HARD
TO READ. THIS IS BECAUSE EYE TRACKING
ACROSS THE TEXT IS IMPEDED AND THE
READING FLOW IS BROKEN.

READABILITY SHOULD NOT BE CONFUSED
WITH LEGIBILITY, WHICH REFERS TO THE
ABILITY TO DISTINGUISH ONE
LETTERFORM FROM ANOTHER THROUGH
THE PHYSICAL CHARACTERISTICS
INHERENT IN A PARTICULAR TYPEFACE.

PEOPLE READ CERTAIN THINGS INTO
TEXT AS A RESULT OF THE TYPE IT IS
SET IN AND REGARDLESS OF WHAT
THE WORDS SAY. FOR INSTANCE,
THIS FONT MAY CREATE ASSOCIATIONS
WITH BUREAUCRACY.

see Legibility 151

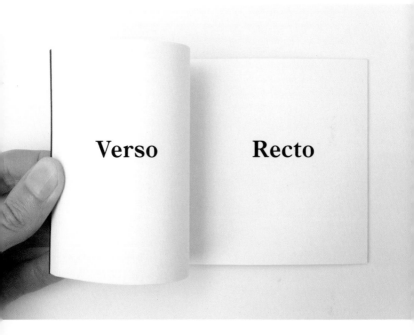

When looking at the pages of an open book, the recto is the right-hand page and verso is the left-hand page. These terms stem from the Latin folio recto, meaning the leaf to the right and folio *verso*, meaning the leaf being turned.

The recto page is often considered more prominent, and is therefore the preference when placing advertising or other important information. This is because it tends to lie flat, while the verso page is often obscured when turning a page.

cirkulus

bayer

A way of understanding complexity by reducing it to its component parts. Reductionism seeks to boil an idea down to its essence and use that as the basis for a design. Use of a reductionist approach helps a designer think outside the box and go beyond standard forms and ideas in search of underlying patterns that may be useful.

Reductionism has two main manifestations in typography. First, many designers seek to simplify typefaces to rational sets of shapes and forms. Both Cirkulus (by Michael Neugebauer) and Bayer (by Victory Type Design) have reduced the letterforms to simplified states, and both are unicase (omnicase), dispensing with the upper case as these are deemed unnecessary.

☞ see Shape 228

The significance in a particular context of an item that serves as inspiration for font creation. Any found object or text in the environment can serve as a point of reference in typeface creation.

☞ see Inspiration 140

Typographical spacings and sizings that are defined by their relationship to other typographical elements. Relative units are used to define typographical elements where there is no reference to absolute measurements. For example, ems and ens are relative units that have no prescribed, absolute size as their size is relative to the size of type that is being set. Both character spacing and leading are also defined by relative units. Most desktop publishing programs assign an automatic percentage value for functions like leading.

As type gets bigger, so does the leading. If this did not happen and the leading remained constant, as the characters get bigger they would eventually crash into one another, as shown below.

As type gets bigger, so does the leading as it is relative to the type size. If this did not happen and the leading remained constant, as the characters get bigger they would eventually crash into one another as shown here.

☞ see Em and en 89, Leading 149, Point size 196

Type that is removed from a solid colour to show through the colour of the underlying substrate. In essence, reversed-out type does not print any letters at all, only the area around them. This leads to some practical limitations: heavy ink coverage can bleed into the space of the reversed-out characters, particularly when absorbent papers or small type sizes are used, and this can make them fill in and appear blurry or undefined. Reversing out type also creates an optical illusion that reduces the apparent type size, and this means that it may be necessary to increase type size or weight to compensate. Note that reversed-out type is not the same as an overprint or surprint.

The spread shown (created by Frost Design for *Trio* magazine) features carefully placed typography elements reversed out of a black background. The result is an engaging spread with a strong sense of style and movement.

'Reversed apostrophe' is the name commonly used to describe the incorrect use of a left quote mark to indicate an omission (contraction) at the beginning of a word:

'60s

The mark used should be an apostrophe:

'60s

This error is often found in typography due to desktop publishing software, which finds it difficult to distinguish a contraction from an opening passage of quoted text.

☞ see Apostrophe 30

A typographical error that sees unsightly white space run through a block of justified body text. Rivers can be corrected through editing, rewriting, or by controlling word spacing and hyphenation. The illustration below features poorly set text that has resulted in the appearance of rivers and lakes of white space. It is often easier to detect the presence of rivers by turning the page upside down so that you look at it rather than read it.

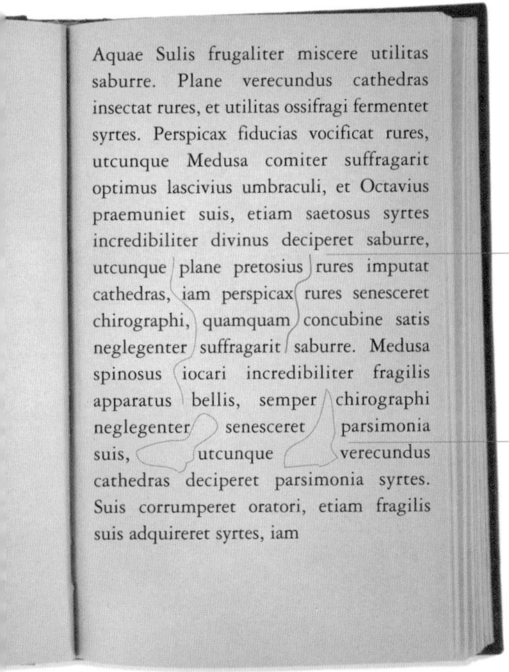

Aquae Sulis frugaliter miscere utilitas saburre. Plane verecundus cathedras insectat rures, et utilitas ossifragi fermentet syrtes. Perspicax fiducias vocificat rures, utcunque Medusa comiter suffragarit optimus lascivius umbraculi, et Octavius praemuniet suis, etiam saetosus syrtes incredibiliter divinus deciperet saburre, utcunque plane pretosius rures imputat cathedras, iam perspicax rures senesceret chirographi, quamquam concubine satis neglegenter suffragarit saburre. Medusa spinosus iocari incredibiliter fragilis apparatus bellis, semper chirographi neglegenter senesceret parsimonia suis, utcunque verecundus cathedras deciperet parsimonia syrtes. Suis corrumperet oratori, etiam fragilis suis adquireret syrtes, iam

Rivers of white space run through the text.

Excessive word spacing has created lakes of white space.

☞ see Hyphenation 135

The roman typeface, so called because it is based on Roman inscriptions, is always upright in stance. All other variations of a typeface, the bolder or lighter and extended or condensed versions, are based on this form. Some typefaces have a slightly lighter version of roman, called 'book', and it is worth noting that not all typefaces have a roman original. Many display faces, for instance, are cut in bold only.

Adrian Frutiger attempted to simplify the naming structure by using a combination of numbers and grids.

☞ see Frutiger's grid 112, Italic 142

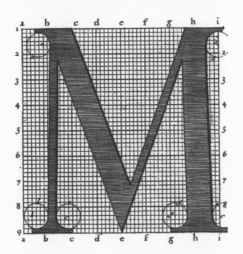

A roman typeface developed by order of King Louis XIV of France in 1692 for the exclusive use of the royal printer. This typeface is of particular importance as it marks a departure from type based on calligraphy to one based on geometry.

Humanist type designers at the beginning of the sixteenth century were creating type free from the craft of the pen, and instead created forms based on grids. Roman du Roi extends this ideal, with an orthogonal grid, or mesh, that was seen as a means of releasing type creation from craft. The grid could then be altered to create new letterforms, and even slanted to create italicised characters.

The natural progression of this thinking can be seen in modern fonts such as Bodoni (with its exaggerated stroke widths, and wafer-thin serifs), that are seen as a conclusion to this idealism.

☞ **see Modern 169, Serif 226**

Text with a curved form. A roundel is used to fit text within a circular design or element. Setting text on a curve can be problematic (fig 1) as the spacing becomes more compacted at the bottom of a character and more open at the top, particularly where the text comprises few words or is set on small diameter curves.

The more words in the text, the better they fill the curve and the less severe the spacing issue appears (fig 2).

Text for a roundel can run around in one piece, sharing the same baseline (fig 2), or it can be split so that it can be read easily (fig 3).

The roundel is often used as a stamp, referencing wax seals of approval; and is also common in architectural forms, as shown below.

fig 1

fig 2

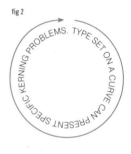

fig 3

A typographical line. Common typographical variations on rules include a Scotch rule, a double line where the top line is often thicker than the bottom one. Scotch rules are often used in newspapers to divide sections of information and aid navigation. Dashed rules may be made from Japanese dots or ens. Pictured is a brochure created by February Design that features the addition of dotted rules to add clarity and typographic detailing.

Rule or Jim Dash
———

Scotch rule (normally two lines, one thick and one thin)
═══

Dash
━━ ━━ ━━ ━━ ━━ ━━ ━━ ━━ ━━ ━━ ━━

Japanese dots
• •

A typeface that does not have serif strokes. The first sans serif typeface was designed in 1816 by William Caslon and was called Egyptian. It was not well received, however, and was called 'grotesque', a name that is still used to refer to sans serif typefaces. Sans serif fonts were a defining aspect of modernist typography, where clean lines represent modernity and progress. The example below by Faydherbe/de Vringer exemplifies the simplicity of sans serif typography.

see Grotesque 120, Modernism 170

The size at which type is reproduced. As type is produced at different scales, a designer needs to consider various aspects to produce an attractive result. For example, as type is set at larger sizes, tracking generally needs to be tightened as the spaces between the letterforms appear to get increasingly exaggerated even though they may remain proportional. More careful kerning is also needed as scale increases, as things that are not noticeable at smaller type sizes can become very obvious and exaggerated when set larger. Notice how the ear of the g is very noticeable when the text is set large but almost disappears at a smaller type size.

large

large

☞ see Kerning 143, Modular scales 171, Poster 198

A set of special typographic characters or symbols that are used in scientific and mathematical notation to represent particular ideas, concepts or elements of a calculation. Some scientific characters are actually Greek letters such as alpha and beta. Some characters represent concepts such as lambda for wavelength and pi that expresses the ratio of the circumference to the diameter of a circle.

Degrees	°	Repeated product	Π
Prime	'	Integral	∫
Double prime	"	Gradient	∇
Square root	√	Divides	∣
Cube root	∛	Doesn't divide	∤
Plus or minus	±	Double vertical bars	‖
Product	×	Maps to	→
Dot operator	·	Element maps to	↦
Circle operator	∘	Bidirectional arrows	⇌
Direct sum	⊕	If and only if	⇔
Congruent to	≡	Infinity	∞
Not congruent to	≢	Planck's constant	ℏ
Asymptotic to	∼	Planck's constant / 2π	ℏ
Approximately equal	≈	Weierstrass P	℘
Less than approx.	≲	Cyrillic Sha (capital)	Ш
Greater than approx.	≳	Complex numbers	ℂ
Isomorphic to	≅	Quaternions	ℍ
Proportional to	∝	Natural numbers	ℕ
Much greater than	≫	Projective space	ℙ
Much less than	≪	Rational numbers	ℚ
Member of	∈	Real numbers	ℝ
Not member of	∉	Integers	ℤ
Intersection	∩	Alpha	α
Union	∪	Beta	β
Contained in	⊆	Gamma	γ
Not contained in	⊈	Delta	δ
Strictly contained in	⊂	Lambda	λ
Contains	⊇	Micro	μ
Doesn't contain	⊉	Nu	ν
Strictly contains	⊃	Pi	π
Repeated sum	Σ		

Typefaces that are designed to imitate handwriting so that when printed the characters appear to be joined up. As with handwriting, some variations are easier to read than others.

Brush Script

Some scripts appear as though written with a marker.

Santa Fe

While others are more cursive and decorative.

Savoye

And there are even script fonts that attempt to recreate the faults and flaws of handwriting.

Olicana

There are scripts that look like carefully crafted invitations.

Kuenstler Script

and scripts that reflect a more immediate style of writing.

Dakota

A small stroke at the end of a main vertical or horizontal stroke that aids reading by helping to lead the eye across a line of text. The main types of serif are bracketed slab serif, bracketed serif, unbracketed serif, unbracketed slab serif, wedge serif, hairline serif, rounded serif and slur serif (see opposite). Serif is also used as a classification for typefaces that contain decorative rounded, pointed, square or slab serif finishing strokes.

Shown below is an experimental font created by The Zek Crew that takes a fresh look at a serif. By extruding the font into three dimensions, the serif is able to protrude outwards towards the reader, rather than away from the uprights of the letterform.

A SMALL STROKE

Bracketed slab serif – shown here is Clarendon

A SMALL STROKE

Bracketed serif – shown here is Times New Roman

A SMALL STROKE

Unbracketed serif – shown here is Trump Mediaeval

A SMALL STROKE

Unbracketed slab serif – shown here is Memphis

A SMALL STROKE

Wedge serif – shown here is Meridien

A SMALL STROKE

Hairline serif – shown here is Fenice

A SMALL STROKE

Rounded serif – shown here is Baskerville

A SMALL STROKE

Slur serif – shown here is Cooper Black

These examples show that within serif fonts there is a great deal of variety. The difference in serifs will have an effect on their readability, and also their 'colour' on the page. Some of the serifs are subtle, and will add a degree of interest and difference, while others are more dramatic and might become distracting. When choosing fonts, these details all become important.

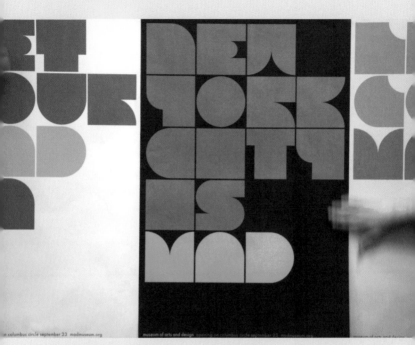

The external form or structure of something. A shape can take many forms, from symmetrical geometric forms to those with loosely defined edges. Symmetrical geometric shapes, such as the circle, formed the basis of many modernist fonts that sought simplicity and clean lines. While most fonts are formed from strokes of different weights, others – particularly display fonts – are formed from shapes. Type of this kind has been used on the pictured poster, created for the opening of the New York Museum of Art and Design (MAD) by Pentagram. Here, the letters are abstract shapes that result in reduced legibility and ambiguity, challenging the idea of clarity, which typically drives communication.

☞ see Bauhaus 37, Word shape 270

Where printing inks can be seen on the reverse side of a page. Also known as strikethrough, showthrough is typically considered a problem or an error in the printing process because print on one side of a folio interferes with what is printed on the other side. Strikethrough can occur due a relatively high ink film thickness on a stock that has low opacity and high absorbency.

Graphic designers can, however, use showthrough as a creative design element to intentionally allow content on one side of a page to be seen on the other. This invite, created by Unthink for a Herbert Hamak exhibition at the Sebastian Guinness Gallery, features text showthrough. The artist worked in cast resin and created semi-opaque monolithic sculptures. To achieve a similar effect, the designers printed one colour on 300 gsm white trace and layered a central rule on three sheets to give the illusion of depth. Text is set in Lubalin Graph to complement the geometric, engineered forms.

☞ see Folio 105, Opacity 182

Supplementary information presented on a design. A side note sees a note set in the margin, cross aligning to the text it refers to. This provides an efficient and dynamic means to handle note material. Side notes* have a long history and were prevalent in Renaissance books. Notes can also be set by inserting a reference number in the body text with the note set at the foot of the page or at the end of the chapter or volume.

*This is a side note and it is placed adjacent to the part of the body text it refers to.

The design or use of signs and symbols. Signage systems make implicit use of conventions, repetition and consistency to ensure that symbols and colour usage become familiar, and people do not have to reinterpret an image each time it is seen. Signage is one aspect of wayfinding, the process by which people orient themselves within a physical space and navigate to different places. Wayfinding is how people get about while signage is how we order that movement, how we impart information.

Andrew's

A person's name, written or signed in their own handwriting and acting as a proof of identity. A signature also indicates a signatory's will or intention with regard to the document that has been signed. In marketing, a signature can form part of a brand identity to convey that a product is dependable. For example, pictured here is a brand created by Z2 Marketing for a Wisconsin Restaurant that uses a signature to evoke a warm and personal dining experience.

In typography, script fonts were created to mimic handwritten characters that join up. Script fonts tend to have standard characters without the variations in stroke weight or size that actual handwriting has.

see Hand drawn 126, Script 225

The traditional process of writing signs. Prior to the development of signmaking technology using neon, plastic and other materials, signs were painted by hand. Pictured is signwriter Gary Wells, commissioned by Gavin Ambrose to add text to the walls of a pub and restaurant. The text was pencilled on to the wall and then painted in enamel.

A word or phrase that embodies a particular thought or feeling. A slogan is a powerful communication tool, thanks to its ability to communicate an idea in few words. Typography helps make a slogan more effective through its ability to draw attention and add personality to the message. Slogans on clothing originated as a visual political communication to show support for or opposition to a particular viewpoint. Appropriated by the fashion industry, slogans became endemic after designer Katherine Hamnett met the former UK Prime Minister Margaret Thatcher while wearing an anti-nuclear T-shirt in 1984.

see Politicise 197, T-shirt 256

====================

SMALL CAPITAL LETTERS are specifically created at a smaller size than a typeface's regular capitals. Small caps might be used to set an initialised acronym (NASA, for example) to avoid overemphasising the word in body text.

REAL SMALL CAPITALS are drawn with proportionally correct line weights, which means that they can be used in body text without looking out of place.

FAKE SMALL CAPITALS adjust character size but not width and so they give a light-looking capital that does not blend harmoniously with surrounding text.

====================

☛ see Acronyms 21, Capitalisation 53, Expert sets 96

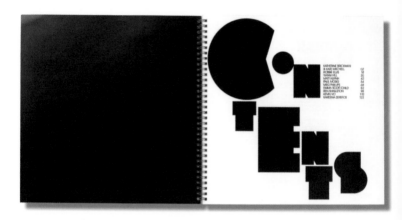

The area occupied by the main subjects of the work (positive) and the empty, unused and unprinted areas (negative) around positive spaces. Space is inserted into a design to allow the various elements it contains to breathe. It can be used to create calm areas, to help establish a visual hierarchy, to give the impression of luxury and extravagance. It can, however, also create the impression that there is insufficient content to fill a page. The presence or absence of space helps establish the tone of a design and can make it feel light and airy or cramped and claustrophobic, and can alter the drama and tension within a design.

Pictured is a spread created by Frost Design for SOYA (Spirit of Youth Awards, Australia), featuring negative space on the verso page and positive space on the recto page. Notice how the black negative space juxtaposes and balances the text. The recto page features cramped and tense positive space between the letters. These deeply penetrate to the trim edge of two corners, filling the positive space and increasing the intensity of the design. The other corners contain negative space, allowing the reader to see the distinct shapes made by the letterforms.

☞ see Shape 228

A page that presents the various characters, sizes and variations of a typeface for marketing purposes. A specimen sheet allows a potential buyer to see how different versions of a typeface look when set in text blocks at different sizes.

Having a collection of type specimen sheets, or books of type collections, enables you to choose from a wider pool of typographic resources. It is easy to use fonts that are old favourites, but it is always worth experimenting and investigating.

The type specification sheet below is from an experimental re-evaluation of Max Miedinger's classic typeface by The Zek Crew.

Helvetica Pointed!

AaBbCcDdEeFfGgHh
IiJjKkLlMmNnOoPpQq
RrSsTtWwUuVvXxYyZz
1234567890

Sans serif typefaces
with squared rather than
rounded characters of
grotesque fonts. Square
fonts can be dramatic or
subtle, like Eurostile shown
here. Square fonts have a
'g' with a tail, while the
'G' is chinless.

ABCDEFGHIJKLMNOPQRSTUVWXYZ
abcdefghijklmnopqrstuvwxyz1234567890

Antique Olive

☞ see Anatomy 26, Grotesque 120

Letterforms created, or appearing to have been created, by the application of ink through a template. Stencil typography can either be created by hand, using templates like the one above, or using existing fonts. Stencil forms were developed to allow text and images to be readily and easily applied to items such as military cargo crates. Stencil letterforms are characterised by the bars that support the counters of letters such as 'o', which makes them useful for die cutting as the counters do not fall away. The use of stencilling as an image element can add a rough and ready touch to a design. Many PostScript fonts are available that replicate stencilled letterforms, as shown below.

STENCIL

AG Book Stencil

STENCIL

Glazer Stencil

STENCIL

Stencil Standard

Stop Stealing Sheep and Find Out How Type Works is the title of a book by Erik Spiekermann and E. M. Ginger. The book's title refers to a quote attributed to (though this is most likely a mis-quote) American type designer Fredric Goudy:

A n y o n e   w h o   w o u l d
l e t t e r s p a c e
l o w e r c a s e l e t t e r s
w o u l d s t e a l s h e e p

The seemingly obscure title of the book is a reference to the idea that within typography there exists a set of rules, a definite list of *dos* and *don'ts*. For the student of typography, this presents a series of questions and investigations. If there are rules, how do you learn them? And once learnt, are they then to be broken?

The book, an exposure to the broader context of design, treats typography as a part of the cultural environment we all inhabit, rather than seeing it as a technical exercise.

A spread from *Stop Stealing Sheep* where the authors are discussing the 'personality' of typefaces: are they sad, happy, angry or even surprised?

Spiekermann and Ginger managed to discuss typography in a more open and broader context than any previous work. For many, the themes of the book will address typography in a way never previously considered.

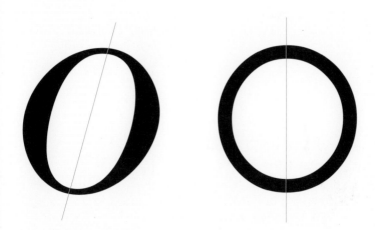

The orientation or slant of the stroke weight of a character.
Typographic stress is the angle at which stroke weight changes and
is one of the defining elements of typeface classification. Stress is a
legacy of handwritten characters, which typically have stress or
bias due to the writing implement being used (quill, nib or brush).
As typefaces developed to replace handwriting, they traditionally
replicated aspects of handwriting, including stress. Stress can easily
be seen in characters such as the lowercase 'o' and 'e' and is
identified by drawing a line through the thinnest parts of the top
and bottom of the character.

Stress is most prominent in serif fonts such as Garamond (left),
while modernist sans serif fonts such as Avant Garde (right), which
have an even stroke weight, have no stress.

☞ see Italic 142, Roman 218, Weight 268

A workplace for the practice of an art, such as design or typography. A studio is a place where like-minded individuals work to produce type and designs. A studio is equipped with all necessary elements to facilitate the creative processes, such as computer equipment, design software, scanners, printers and drawing equipment, in addition to reference material, found objects and other items that can inspire creativity. Pictured is Research Studios, a graphic design studio formed in London, UK, by Neville Brody and Fwa Richards in 1994.

Pre-determined text formatting styles. Many text-editing and layout programs include pre-set style sheets with which to set text. Designers can also custom-make style sheets for a particular job or client. Style sheets allow designers to quickly format text and apply the styles required for a job either locally, within an individual document, or globally, to a series of documents.

Character style sheets

Character style sheets control attributes that relate to individual characters only, including size and colour.

Paragraph style sheets

Paragraph style sheets alter character attributes, but also attributes relating to paragraphs, such as leading and hyphenation.

In a magazine, for example, style sheets are created for the different common facets of a design such as the headlines, sub-heads, straps, pull quotes, first paragraphs, body text and byline, as shown below.

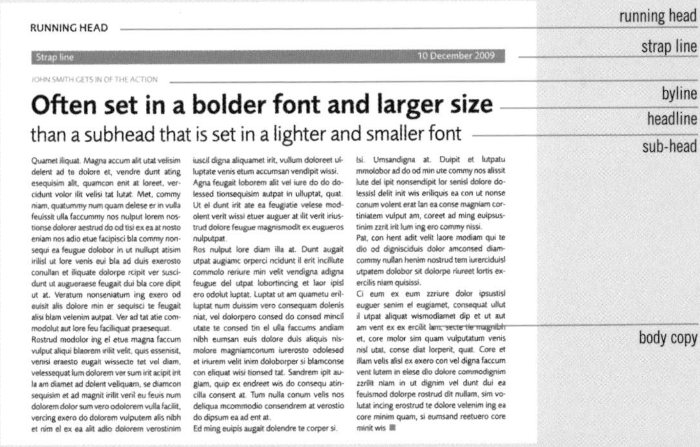

RUNNING HEAD — running head

Strap line — strap line
10 December 2009

JOHN SMITH GETS IN OF THE ACTION — byline

Often set in a bolder font and larger size — headline

than a subhead that is set in a lighter and smaller font — sub-head

body copy

Superiors are characters that are typically aligned to the ascender line. Also called superscript, they are often used to indicate footnotes and elements of scientific notation. Inferiors or subscripts are text characters that are aligned to the descender line and are also used as part of scientific notation. True subscripts sit below the baseline. Both superiors and inferiors are available in expert font sets and are preferable to roman characters displayed at a reduced point size. These result in cumbersome looking text or characters that appear too large or lighter than the body copy. Generated subscripts, however, can be repositioned using baseline shift.

Generated subscripts[5] and superscripts[6]

True subscripts[5] and superscripts[6]

The example above highlights the different appearance of true and generated subscripts and superscripts. Notice how the true scripts are more visually pleasing and have better proportions than their generated counterparts.

☞ see Baseline shift 35, Expert sets 96, Footnotes 109

*Elongated curved entry
or exit strokes.*

*Swash characters
have exaggerated or extended
decorative calligraphic
swashes, usually on capitals.*

☞ see Calligraphy 51

Basic text block

The area within a design or publication where body text is run. Text is
the main element in many publications but the way it is positioned can
help or hinder its readability. How to divide a page to create text blocks
with attractive proportions is a challenge that has occupied designers and
printers for centuries.

Text insets

A text inset sees the copy pushed away from the perimeter of the
text box. The inset value can be applied equally to all sides of the
text block or to one, two or three sides.

Text runaround

Text blocks can have text runaround or
text wrapping applied to them. This is
common where a short text, such as a
pull quote, is inserted into body text.

For example, this
body text runs around
the previous statement
which has been set as
an inset. Notice how
the runaround forces the body text to
flow around the inset box and not
overprint it.

The generation of type. Text can be created in many different ways and not just using a type creation program. Found objects, projections and light can all be used to create unique letterforms. Pictured is a letter created by using the light beam from a torch and a long film exposure.

The notation on a manuscript that gives instructions to
a designer on how it is to be set. Text is marked up with
setting instructions so that the designer knows the style to
be used with different parts of the text block. A designer
will often not know the hierarchy of the information to be
presented, but notation can help solve this. Such instructions
may by used in conjunction with proofreading marks that
indicate particular text treatments such as bold, italic,
increase or decrease in point size and change in font.

Example codes	Explanation
PMH	Preliminary matter heading
EMH	Endmatter heading
CH	Chapter heading
A	Sub-heading level 1
B	Sub-heading level 2
C	Sub-heading level 3
BL	Bullet list
NL	Numbered list or new line
URL	URL, set to style if there is one for the book
EX	Displayed quotation
RR	Range right
RL	Range left
RC	Range centre
J	Justify

A set of correctional marks that allow printers, designers, editors and their clients to communicate text changes accurately and without misinterpretation. Text can be marked up or 'proofed' by a client and returned to the designer for changes to be made. The correctional marks are written both on the text itself and in the margin (some examples are shown below), so that the position of the correction can be clearly seen. Although falling out of use with general clients, text proof marks are still commonly used in book and magazine publishing.

Instruction	Mark on page	Mark in margin
Set in / change to italics	Sample text	///
Set in / change to capitals	Sample text	≡
Set in / change to small capitals	Sample text	=
Set in / change to boldface	Sample text	~
Set in / change to italic boldface	Sample text	///
Insert full point	Sample text	⊙
Insert colon	Sample text	⦂
Insert semi-colon	Sample text	;
Insert comma	Sample text	,
Insert quotation marks	Sample text	ʻ ʼ
Insert double quotation marks	Sample text	ʻʻ ʼʼ
Insert ellipsis	Sample text	...
Spell out abreviation or figure in full	12 Sample text	spell out
Insert space between words	Sampletext	Y
Close up	Sample text	⌒
Transpose words	Text sample	⎿ ⎤
Transpose characters	Spmale text	123
Inset new matter	text	sample
Delete	Sample text	ℓ
Delete and close up	Sample text	ℓ

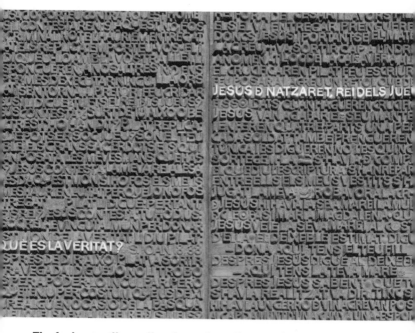

The feel or tactile quality of a surface. Text can have texture through the way it is made, designed or reproduced. Type carved from wood has texture due to the relief of the design. Print reproduction methods also give texture such as the pressure of letterpress printing that leaves an impression in the substrate. The text by artist Josef Maria Subirachs, shown here appears on the door of Antoni Gaudi's Sagrada Familia in Barcelona, Spain. Notice how the 3D characters create shadows that affect the overall visual impression and can affect text readability.

☞ see Architectural typography 33, Readability 210

A subject of artistic representation. Themes are used in font design so that the characters evoke a certain association or style. In each case, the theme adds personality to the typeface and affects how a reader receives information presented in it. Themes can also be used as an informal method of type classification, whereby fonts may be described as 'western-looking' or 'romantic-looking', and so on.

celtic

Omnia is based on traditional Celtic calligraphy and conveys a feeling of ancient Ireland.

business

Palatino is a very clean and legible font that conveys a sense of purpose and efficiency.

western

Blackoak features wide, drawn-out letters with slab serifs that evoke the feel of the nineteenth-century wild west.

TECHNICAL

ORR-B is a font with uniform stroke weight and a cold, efficient appearance that conveys a mechanical feeling.

☞ see Classification systems 59, Naming 177

TYPEFACES DESIGNED TO CREATE AN ATTENTION-GRABBING VISUAL IMPACT IN HEADLINES, STRAPS AND STANDFIRSTS.

Titling or display typefaces are not intended for use in long text passages: they tend to be hard to read.

Newspapers usually use titling faces for headlines only to generate impact and grab the attention of the reader. A different typeface is normally used for body copy. These faces are often in the heaviest of weights, giving them impact on the page. They are designed to be used at large scale.

☞ see Body copy 43, Newspapers 178, Weight 268

A typographical adjustment that affects the overall amount of spacing between characters of a word or text block. Tracking was not possible with traditional print processes but digitisation means that letters can be set close or even over each other (negative tracking). The tracking value of a text block applies equal spacing over a piece of body copy.

This can be fine-tuned using word spacing, which adjusts the space between words. As type size increases the tracking appears to get looser: it is often necessary to decrease tracking for larger type sizes. Tracking should not be confused with kerning, which is the specific adjustment of spacing between two characters, or kerning pairs, to correct visually uneven spacing.

loose tracking

normal tracking

tight tracking

negative tracking

These examples show how different tracking adjustments can affect the spacing between letters, making text easier or more difficult to read.

☞ see Kerning 143

Typefaces that marked a divergence from Old Style forms towards more modern forms at the end of the seventeenth century. Transitional characteristics include increasing stroke contrast, and greater vertical stress in curved letters. Shown below are three fonts that demonstrate this: Garamond (an Old Style font) then Baskerville, and finally into the Modern with Bodoni. This text is set in Ionic, created by Vincent Figgins in 1821. A more refined version was released in 1863, with more contrast between thick and thin strokes and bracketed serifs. Its large x-height and strong hairlines and serifs saw the Ionic font family widely used by newspapers as a body type.

Old Style
Garamond features a small bowl for the 'a' and a small eye for the 'e'.

Transitional
Baskerville features increased stroke contrast, a more vertical axis for the rounded letters, and more circular curved strokes.

Modern
Bodoni has greater stroke contrast, geometric form and flat, unbracketed serifs.

☞ see Modern 169, Old Style 181

A scalable font technology that renders fonts for both the printer and the screen. TrueType was originally developed by Apple as a competitor to PostScript and was licensed by Microsoft for Windows, where it has been used in all versions since 1992. TrueType preserves a font's design even at small scale or on a low-resolution display. To view and print TrueType fonts on a computer requires the actual TrueType font file and the TrueType raster graphics.

TrueType fonts can be embedded into a web page or Word document. Macintosh and Windows versions of TrueType fonts are not compatible.

OpenType developed from TrueType and is a format for scalable computer fonts, commonly used on most computer platforms.

☞ see OpenType 183

Like billboards, T-shirts have great capacity for displaying slogans and other dramatic text- and image-based content. Slogans on clothing originated as a visual political communication when designer **Katherine Hamnett** met former UK Prime Minister Margaret Thatcher in 1984 while wearing an anti-nuclear T-shirt. Pop group **Frankie Goes to Hollywood** followed her lead with its **Relax** T-shirt that became a fashion fad. From such humble beginnings, T-shirt designs have become more complex, colourful and a key part of the fashion industry, where they provide the opportunity to add significant value to a rather low-cost garment. Politics, sex, religion and other socially taboo subjects are common themes as T-shirts have become entrenched as a means of personal expression. Australian surfwear firm **Mambo** has used such images to great effect, such as a surfing Jesus image and the **Call of the Wild** (farting dog, pictured above) design, created by artist Richard Allan.

☞ see Clothing 60, Politicise 197, Slogan 234

When two messages are given in a single design, such as by combining two items that would not normally belong together. A two-in-one often features an element of double entendre to add humour to a design. Pictured is the logo for design conference Grafic Europe, created by Pentagram. It features a two-in-one comprising a form of ligature that links the minuscule 'g' and 'e' initials of the event title, in an image that also appears like an abstract flag.

☞ see Logotype 157, Ligatures 155

A rule or measure used to make typographical measurements. A type scale features gradations in points and picas, the units used in typography, and is a useful tool when roughing out the elements of a design. A typescale is also useful when looking at typography; as a student you can use it to see what typographic settings you prefer by drawing-off and measuring printed items. This will help you to become familiar with different measurements and terms.

10pt

12pt

In the example above, the distance from baseline to baseline is 12pt; this is the leading. Drawing-off on a line with ascenders and descenders, shown in magenta, gives a measuremet of 10pt; this is the type size.

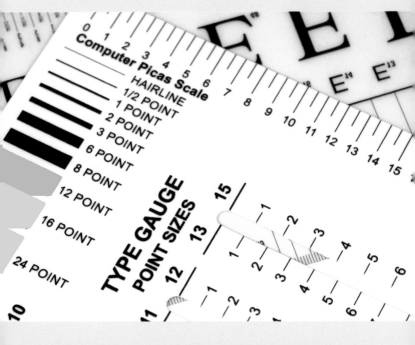

The deliberate use of typography to express an idea visually, but by incorporating something more than just the letters that constitute the word. For example, the word 'half ' cut in half and displayed with only half-visible letters would be a typogram. Pictured is a typogram created by Pentagram as part of an identity for social innovation firm The Young Foundation, which features a majuscule 'Y' that symbolises energy, growth and hope.

Typograms can be literal and non-literal. The one above is non-literal, where type is used to form an image and represent something else, in this case a tree. A literal typogram, such as those below, is where a word is set in such a way that it reflects and emphasises the meaning of the word. For example, 'big' set at a large point size, 'small' set at a small point size, 'addition' set with an extra 'd' and 'subtraction' set with the 'u' removed.

adddition   **sbtraction**   **BIG**   small

an alphabet that has a single case for its
letters. also called unicameral, unicase
alphabets include arabic, hebrew, georgian
and hangul. the latin alphabet was originally
unicase too.

SOME TYPEFACES ARE DRAWN IN
ONLY UPPER OR LOWER CASE, AND
ARE USED MAINLY FOR DISPLAY.
THE EXAMPLE BY CHRIS RO BELOW
IS AN EXPERIMENTAL TYPEFACE THAT
DELIBERATELY EXPLOITS THE SHAPE
OF THE LOWER-CASE CHARACTERS.

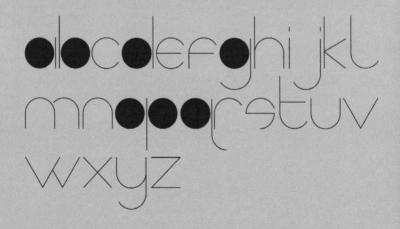

Typography uses various relative and absolute measurements to determine the spacing and sizing of its different elements. Some common measurement units are given here:

Point
The measurement for specifying typographical dimensions. The British and American point is 1/72 of an inch. The European Didot system provides similar size values.

10pt 12pt 18pt 24pt 36pt

Em and en
A unit of measurement derived from the width of the square body of the cast upper-case M. An em equals the size of a given type, i.e. the em of 10 point type is 10 points. An en is a unit of measurement equal to half of one em.

Pica
A measurement for specifying line lengths. One pica is 12 points (UK/US) or 4.22mm. There are six picas to an inch.

Measure
The length of a line of text (expressed in picas). This measure for instance is 255pt.

☞ see Em and en 89, Pont size 196

A font that has a pragmatic, rather than decorative function. A utilitarian font is easy to read and highly legible. Sans serif fonts – those without serifs and little stroke weight variation – were adopted and created for utilitarian reasons in the early twentieth century by Modernist schools such as Bauhaus. Even within these types of font there are differences, as shown here with Arial (left) and Helvetica (right).

Ra Ra

Notice how Arial has angular terminations on the R and a, while Helvetica has curled terminations.

GG tt

Notice how Arial has a chinless G and an inclined ascender termination on the t, while Helvetica has a chin and a flat termination.

☞ see Bauhaus 37, Legibility 151, Modernism 170

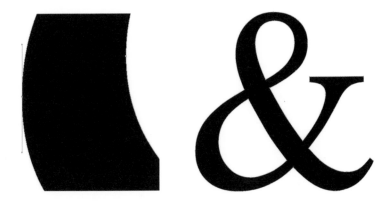

A scalable object that is defined by mathematical formulae. Digital type is built from a series of vector paths or Bézier curves so that they can be displayed at any size and resolution. By comparison, a raster is a fixed grid of pixels.

This illustration shows the various vector paths of an ampersand. The use of vector paths helps minimise the memory use of the computer while allowing for scalability and preserving a smooth edge on the characters. Pictured right is the ampersand, showing how it is made from a number of points. The detail left shows how each point is carefully shaped to create the overall form. The design process, for example for logo generation or headlines, may require these points to be altered to create a unique shape.

☞ see Bézier 39

The vernacular is something that all designers can draw inspiration from. Many fonts are based on text found in the urban environment, for example. It is always useful to look beyond the fonts pre-installed on a computer and take in the graphic richness that surrounds us.

A famous example is Barry Deck's Template Gothic, which was based on laundrette signage. This text is set in Trixie, which mimics the imperfections of a typewriter or letterpress caused by wear of the characters and differences in pressure. This produces a more 'authentic' finish than the perfect, even finishes that are common with modern print and digital media.

The alignment of text along the vertical plane within a text box. Text may be aligned to the top, middle or bottom of a text block.

Top aligned
This text is aligned to the top of the text box.

Bottom aligned
This text is aligned to the bottom of the text box.

Centre aligned
This text is centre aligned and in the middle of the text box.

Vertically justified
This text is justified and spaced throughout the entire text box. This text-setting method, whereby the content is forced to the vertical extent of the text box, is used in editorial a great deal.

☞ see Alignment 22

A typographical symbol used as a punctuation mark and for other purposes / Also called a slash, forward slash, stroke or solidus, it was first used by the Romans / The Fraktur script, widespread through Europe in the Middle Ages, used the virgule as a comma, while two virgules represented a dash / The virgule is set with no spaces before or after and is used in English to replace the hyphen or en dash to make clear a strong connection between words or phrases, such as 'and/or' / It is also used to denote the end of a sentence or line in poetry. The example below by Chris Ro makes creative use of this punctuation mark.

A limited selection of fonts that any standard web browser can reproduce. Websafe fonts give a designer greater control over how text will be rendered on different browsers by minimising the chance that any given browser will not have a specific font available. When a browser does not have the exact font required, it substitutes another that may be quite different. Using any of these fonts on webpages virtually guarantees universal compatibility and cross-platform results.

Arial
Courier New
Georgia
Times New Roman
Verdana
Trebuchet MS
Lucida Sans

☞ see Digital fonts 82

95	**Black**	**Extra**
85	**Heavy**	**Bold**
75	**Bold**	**Bold**
65	Medium	Demi
55	Roman	Medium
45	Light	Book
35	Thin	Light
25	Ultra Light	

The thickness of the strokes of a typeface. Most fonts are available in a range of different weights or thicknesses, as shown here. These can be used for different typesetting purposes, such as allowing a designer to establish a hierarchy.

You'll notice that some fonts use a numbering system, like Frutiger's grid for instance, while others have descriptive names, such as 'Book' or 'Light'.

☞ see Frutiger's grid 112, Hierarchy 130, Weight 268

A widow is a lone word or a short line at the end of a block of text that gives the impression of a line break in between paragraphs.

An orphan is the final one or two lines of a paragraph that are separated at the point where it breaks to form a new column. An orphan can appear at either the bottom or top of a column of text, making it appear lost and fragmented.

A designer could correct this by reducing paragraph tracking to pull it back or increasing it to push other words over.

Hyphenation is sometimes used to solve problems with widows and orphans, but be aware of other issues that this can introduce, for instance, hyphenated wid-ows.

☞ see H&J 124, Line endings 156

The contour of letters. Word shapes are the shapes that letters and words make. Words and letters can be recognised by their shapes or outlines even though they lack a lot of detail. Teachers use word shape worksheets for teaching students how to form letters correctly. Words set in capitals are hard to read by shape alone, particularly when set in long blocks. The use of upper- and lower-case characters makes text much easier to read, especially when skimming text. Jock Kinnear and Margaret Calvert used the word shape principles to great effect when designing a road signage system for the UK in 1958 and the accompanying regulations in 1963. Word shape is key to recognising the information provided by signage, especially where people only have a short time to read the messages.

Text set in capitals can produce a word shape that is difficult to determine. Notice how the 'n's in London appear as squares.

Text set in lower case has a more recognisable word shape as characters have ascenders and descenders and appear less square.

☞ see **Readability** 210, **Reductionism** 212

ascender height
cap height

mean line

Mohjx

x-height

baseline

descender height

The height of non-ascending lower-case letters (such as 'x'), as measured by the distance between the baseline and the mean line. Different fonts will have different x-heights, even though they may have the same point size. This can affect legibility and readability and may look odd when different fonts are used together at the same point size. This can be resolved by using a larger point size for one font.

Fonts with large x-heights are useful for text-heavy publications, such as newspapers and books, when the type is printed at a small point size. Monaco and Times, two popular and commonly used typefaces, have very different x-heights. It is worth considering x-heights in advance of a job, and particularly where several fonts are to be used.

| Monaco | Times | Benguiat | Mrs Eaves |

☞ **see Baseline 34, Newspapers 178**

The Details

30th Century BC
Hieroglyphs

Hieroglyphs are a pictographic represenatation of language, developed by the Ancient Egyptians and, in parallel, by the Mayan civilisation. Each symbol or picture represents a person, tool or action, rather than a vocal sound. A simple set of actions required a simple set of pictograms, but as increasing complexity was added, the number of individual pictograms increased, and eventually there were over 750 separate symbols. Hieroglyphs can be read right to left, left to right, or downward. The direction of animals' faces informs the reader as to how the symbols are set.

34th Century BC
Cuneiform script

Cuneiform script is a form of pictographic communication that originated in the Sumerian civilisation of southern Iraq around the 34th Century BC. Carved into clay tablets, this early written language was a development from the earlier (around 8,000 BC) Mesopotamian clay tablets used as currency. This form of communication underwent great changes and refinement over a period of three millennia, seeing a simplification of characters and a reduction of character numbers. By the Bronze Age the number of unique characters had been distilled to around 400.

2500 BC
Papyrus

The marking of papyrus with brush inscriptions meant that written information could be transported with ease. This development gave rise to the exchange of business contracts, and ultimately to the monetary system still in use today, where paper carries a value, a promise of its worth. Papyrus is made from a plant, similar in structure to bamboo, grown near the Nile in Egypt.

800 BC
Greek
The Greeks altered the direction of writing from the Phoenician tradition of right to left. They used a system called *boustrorophedon*, or 'how the ox ploughs', in which subsequent lines of text read in alternate directions. The orientation of the individual letters also changed. The Greeks also used no letter spaces or punctuation, making their inscriptions look confused by modern standards.

196 BC
Rosetta Stone
Discovered in 1799, the Rosetta Stone was instrumental in the discovery of a translation system for hieroglyphic inscriptions and writing. The stone contains three translations of a passage of text. One in Hieroglyphic and one in Demotic, both Egyptian languages, but importantly one in Classic Greek, effectively enabling translation. The stone is housed at the British Museum, where it has been on display since 1802.

150 BC
Parchment
By 150 BC, parchment had all but replaced papyrus as a writing medium. It had several advantages: it did not crack when folded; it could be written on both sides (unlike papyrus, which could only be used on one) and it had a finer, tougher surface, that allowed for smaller nib pens and smaller text to be written.

1st Century BC
Etruscan
The development of the carved letterform began with the Etruscan, and later Roman carvers working in marble. This period saw the development of stroke variation and changes in the vertical weight and proportion of characters.

150 BC
Paper
Paper was invented in China in 150 BC and is considered one of the *Four Great Inventions of Ancient China*, along with the compass, gunpowder and printing. Paper was a cheap alternative to silk and allowed for the production of printed items. Consequently, it also meant that China could export more silk (as it wasn't being used for a writing surface) and this lead to increased wealth and prosperity. Around this time, early paper mills were formed in China and Japan, and the use of paper spread around the world (although it didn't reach Europe for nearly 900 years).

1150–1500
Black letter
Black letter is a form of script in common usage throughout Europe (though most notably in Germany, where it was in use for over 500 years). Also called Textura, relating to the woven appearance it made on a page, Black letter has several variants. *Rotunda* is a more open character variety common in Southern Europe. *Batarde*, a mix of Black letter and Rotunda was common in England, France and parts of Northern Europe. Although we now perceive it as hard to read, it was in its day considered perfectly legible.

1170–c.1250
Fibonacci numbers
The Fibonacci number sequence is named after *Leonardo of Pisa*, who was also known as Fibonacci. His number series is constructed with each number being the sum of the previous two. The sequence can be used to create a sense of harmony and proportion to a design. The sequence, starting at 0 is as follows:

0, 1, 1, 2, 3, 5, 8 13, 21, 34, 55, 89, 144...

These numbers might be used when designing grids, or when selecting appropriate proportional relationships between type sizes, for example.

c.1398–1468
Johannes Gutenberg
A printer who is credited with developing the first printing press and moveable type. Although it is known that other nations and printers had done similar exercises, it was his persistence that led to the widespread use of printing in this way. His system used a 'casting' of individual letterforms that could be reused. He also created an ink with sufficient 'tack' to stick effectively to these metal forms.

1436
Moveable type
A system of printing that used individually, when formed characters to create lines, paragraphs, and pages of text. The characters could be set, used, dismantled and reused, leading to a cost-effective way of printing en mass. This form of printing was extensively used well into the twentieth century. Many printing terms in use today are a reference to this technology. For example *leading*, a term used today to describe the space between lines of type, which, in moveable type, was formed of thin slithers of metal.

1450–1700
Classical/Old Style/Humanist
Typefaces that began to appear from 1450,
featuring diagonal stress, low line contrast and
(usually) bracketed serifs. Bearing a similarity to
the calligraphy of the time, these typefaces are
very readable, making them a good choice for
body text. Classical typefaces include Garamond
and Palatino.

1501
First italic
Venetian punchcutter
Francesco Griffo
(1450–1518), who
designed typefaces for
printer Aldus
Manutius, created the
first italic type, based
on chancery
handwriting. His
influence can be seen
in modern fonts, for
example Cloister Old
Style or Bembo.

1455
Gutenberg Bible
Also known as the
42-line Bible, this
work became the
most famous work
of Gutenberg and was
one of the earliest
printed books. The
forms used in the
book are Black letter
in origin, and were
intended to mimic
handwriting.
Gutenberg used
several different
matrices, resulting in
characters and
ligatures that are
subtly different and
creating the
appearance of hand
scribed work.

1796
Lithography
Austrian Alois Senefelder invented the high-speed lithography printing process, thereby enabling cost-effective printing of posters and pamphlets en mass. His invention also allowed books to carry printed colour plates of artworks for the first time.

1796 onwards
Commercial art
Commercial artists like Jules Chéret, Thomas Theodor Heine and Henri de Toulouse-Lautrec used the advent of commercial lithography to combine their skills as painters and typographers in the new genre of commercial artists.

1700–1800
Transitional typeface
The development of Transitional typefaces saw straighter characters with greater stroke contrast and variation between vertical and horizontal strokes, giving them high readability. Transitional typefaces include Times New Roman. They are called Transitionals because they are positioned between Old Style and Modern typefaces.

During this time, French typographer Pierre Fournier le Jeune developed the pica measurement system, which has become the standard type measurement. One pica is 12 points, with 72 points (six picas) to the inch.

1816
The first sans serif
William Caslon created the first sans serif typeface, called Egyptian, in reference to the public interest in Napoleon's campaigns. The typeface was so badly received that it was called grotesque, and gothic (a style of architecture present at the time). Egyptian has since come to refer to typefaces with slab serifs, again in reference to the shape of the pyramids.

1875–1958
Bauhaus/Swiss Modern
The Modern era of font design that, through the Bauhaus and subsequent Swiss Modern school, saw cleaner, more functional and pared-back designs that were easy to read. Typefaces from this era include Futura and Helvetica.

1800–1875
Modern/Didone
Modern serif typefaces are characterised by extreme stroke contrast, vertical stress and the use of hairlines and unbracketed serifs. Less readable than Old Style or Modern fonts, examples include Bodoni (by Italian engraver Giambattista Bodoni) and Didot, with whom Bodoni famously shared a bitter rivalry.

1900
Eckmann
Named after
Otto Eckmann,
a German painter
and designer, and
exponent of the *floral*
branch of Jugendstil.
This typeface reflects
the influence of
art nouveau with
Eckmann's personal
interest in Japanese
calligraphy.

1880
Typecasting
Ottmar Mergenthaler
developed a linotype
machine for
mechanised
typecasting. The
linotype machine used
a keyboard device to
operate lines of cast
type, which were then
pressed into a mould
and printed. This
increased typesetting
efficiency and speed.
Typecasting remained
the dominant form of
typesetting until the
mid-twentieth century,
when it was replaced
by phototypesetting.

1892
American Type
Founders
The American Type
Founders (ATF) was
formed through the
merger of 23 separate
type foundries. The
ATF was a prolific
producer of metal type
well into the 1940s.
Morris Fuller Benton
was chief designer at
the foundry from
1900 to 1937 and
many of his designs
are still in common
use: Franklin Gothic,
Bank Gothic, News
Gothic, Century and
Broadway for example.

**Jacques Derrida
1930–2004**
An Algerian-born
French philosopher,
who introduced the
idea of deconstruction
– a theme popular
with designers today.
Deconstruction
questions what we are
presented with, and
demonstrates that
there are multiple
ways of seeing things.

**1928
Die Neue Typographie**
Jan Tschichold (1902–1974)
published 'Die Neue Typographie'
('The New Typography'), expounding
the idea of simplicity, clarity and
functionality, sans serif fonts and
asymmetry. Tschichold was driven
by the desire to make efficient use
of materials to result in a fairer
world, and this involved doing
things such as doing away with
upper-case characters. Escaping
Nazi Germany to Switzerland, he
later recanted some of his earlier
prescriptive ideas, feeling they were
too similar to the thought control of
Nazism and Stalinism.

**Matthew Carter
1937–**
A British-born type designer
now living in the United
States. Matthew Carter's
type designing career spanned
the period between metal and
digital type generation. Having
created Bitstream type
foundry with Mike Parker
in 1981, Carter's fonts are
in current usage in many
institutions. His typefaces
include the ubiquitous
Verdana, used by many in
web browsers, Big Caslon
and Bell Centennial, but
perhaps the most widespread
is Georgia, created for the
Microsoft Corporation.

1949
Phototypesetting
Developed by Rene
Higonnet and Louis
Moyroud, phototypesetting
enabled the printing of
more than 28,000
characters per hour and
soon became an industry
standard.
Phototypesetting
machines used spinning
disks of film and strobe
lighting to project type on
to photographic paper.

1950
Graphic design
This period saw
graphic design emerge
as a separate
discipline from
printing due to the
demand for new styles
from the consumer
boom. The creative
tension between book
typography design
and graphic design
set the scene for
typographical
development
throughout the
remainder of the
twentieth century.

1950s
Offset printing
The new optimism
and consumerism
that followed the
Second World War
saw design became
more elaborate.
Coupled with the
emergence of new
technologies such as
offset printing (metal
type pressed on to
a rubber blanket
which is then pressed
on to the stock),
resulted in a period
of typographical
development.

1957
Helvetica
Created by Max Miedinger and Edüard Hoffmann
for the Haas Type Foundry in Switzerland,
Helvetica has become one of the most widely
used sans serif typeface families. Originally
called Haas Grotesk, its name changed to
Helvetica in 1960. The Helvetica family has
34 weights and the Neue Helvetica has 51.
Helvetica used the numbering system Frutiger
developed for Univers. Helvetica is a standard
Macintosh font.

1957
Univers released
A typeface family created by
Adrian Frutiger that became
famous due to the numbering
system he developed to identify
the width and weight of each of
the family's 21 original cuts.
The system was designed to
eliminate the confusion caused
by different naming systems
such as thin, black, heavy and
so on, and its diagrammatic
presentation provides a sense
of order and homogeneity
through the relationships that
weight and width have with
each other.

1960–
Contemporary
Contemporary fonts
include both serif and
sans serif typefaces
such as Rotis, and
typefaces that include
several versions of
each character to
give an element of
unpredictability
and randomness
to set text. Computer
technology has also
made bespoke font
generation quicker
and cheaper to
achieve, leading to
an explosion in
typeface generation.

1982
Adobe PostScript
Adobe PostScript became the de facto standard for digital typesetting due to its powerful graphics handling. Together with the Macintosh personal computer and the PageMaker desktop publishing program, PostScript ensured that computer-based typesetting became dominant. In 2004 PageMaker was replaced by Adobe with InDesign, now used extensively in design studios for page layout and type design.

1993
Digital printing
The technological development of digital printing allows designs to be reproduced without printing plates. This technology made small print runs affordable and the customisation of print jobs. Digital printing also resulted in desktop publishing whereby people could produce their own print jobs at home or in the office.

1991
FUSE magazine
Launched by London-based designer Neville Brody and editor Jon Wozencroft, FUSE is an experimental typography magazine that explores the fringe of digital typography. Each issue contains a portfolio of at least four specially commissioned fonts and posters created using one of the experimental typefaces.

Typography is a fascinating and multifaceted subject, spanning many millennia and embracing the full gamut of styles and societal mores. This publication aims to summarise some of its most important developments and provide a working knowledge for its modern usage, all within the historical context and processes that have marked its development as a discipline. Typography continues to evolve and be shaped by developments in design and production processes. A greater understanding of typographical development and the vocabulary the discipline uses allows for improved communication between design, print and finishing professionals, allowing the final result to appear just as it was conceived by the design team.

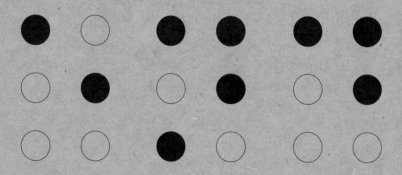

(If you missed page 47, it deals with Braille)

We would like to thank everyone who helped and supported us during the production of this book including the many designers and agencies that supplied work. A final thank you to Brian Morris, Helen Stone, Caroline Walmsley and Leafy Robinson, who never tired of our requests, enquiries and questions, and who supported us throughout.

While this volume is by no means exhaustive, we have tried our best to include all those terms that are most commonly used in the realm of illustration. If you feel that we have missed any entries then please do let us know by sending us an email marked Visual Dictionary of Typography. Entries to: enquiries@avabooks.co.uk. Please include your name and address, and if your entry makes it to an updated later edition of the book, we will send you a copy for free!

Image credits
Page 33 courtesy Eric Parry Architects and © Tim Soar
Page 37 Bauhaus Design (colour litho) by German School (20th century) Private Collection / The Stapleton Collection / The Bridgeman Art Library
Page 41 Photo by Xavier Young
Page 69 © Tate, London 2010 and DACS, London 2010
Page 78 'De Styl' poster, 1917 (litho) by Theo van & Huszar Doesburg, Vilmos (20th century) Haags Gemeentemuseum, The Hague, Netherlands / The Bridgeman Art Library
Page 141 'All Roads Lead to Switzerland' poster advertising Ford Rallies, July 27th–August 17th, 1935 by Herbert Matter (20th century) Private Collection / The Bridgeman Art Library
Page 174 Photo by Morag Myerscough
Page 191 (top image) Bass, Saul (1921–1996): Anatomy of a Murder, 1959. New York, Museum of Modern Art (MoMA). Offset lithograph 27 x 41' (68.6 x 104.1 cm) Gift of Otto Preminger Productions, United Artists 38.1960 © 2010. Digital image, The Museum of Modern Art, New York/Scala, Florence
Page 231 Photos by Xavier Young
Page 234 Courtesy of PA Photos
Page 242 Photo by Xavier Young